# Arbitration and Corruption

## ASA Special Series

---

VOLUME 47

---

*Introduction*

The Swiss Arbitration Association (ASA, Association suisse de l'arbitrage) is Switzerland's leading arbitration organization. With more than a thousand members, it brings together the world's most eminent arbitration practitioners from six continents and 50 + jurisdictions.

Since its foundation in 1974, ASA helps shape the development of international arbitration for the benefit of users worldwide. Its signature Annual Conferences in Zurich and Geneva explore topical issues with high-calibre experts from all over the world. The papers and materials are subsequently published in the ASA Special Series.

*Editors*

Each volume of the ASA Special Series is edited by different editors from among the ASA members and who have been the (co-)organizers of the pertinent ASA Annual Conference or are specialists in a particular topical issue to which a volume is dedicated.

*Objective*

The ASA Special Series are published to foster innovation in and to promote international arbitration globally.

They contain the full edited versions of the papers of the ASA Annual Conferences as well as ad hoc arbitration brochures published by ASA.

*Frequency*

One to two volumes per year, with one volume typically published following the ASA Annual Conference.

*The titles published in this series are listed at the end of this volume.*

# Arbitration and Corruption

Edited by

Andrea Meier
Christian Oetiker

Wolters Kluwer

*Published by:*
Kluwer Law International B.V.
PO Box 316
2400 AH Alphen aan den Rijn
The Netherlands
E-mail: international-sales@wolterskluwer.com
Website: lrus.wolterskluwer.com

*Sold and distributed by:*
Wolters Kluwer Legal & Regulatory U.S.
7201 McKinney Circle
Frederick, MD 21704
United States of America
Email: customer.service@wolterskluwer.com

ISBN 978-94-035-3534-0

e-Book: ISBN 978-94-035-3535-7
web-PDF: ISBN 978-94-035-3540-1

# Programme of the Conference

1. Welcome Address and Introduction to the Conference Topic
   *Andrea Meier & Christian Oetiker*
2. **Panel 1: Corruption – What Does It Really Mean?**
   How to Define Corruption?
   The Costs of Corruption and How to Fight It
   'Red Flags' for Identifying Suspicious Relationships
   Moderator
   *Maxi Scherer*, Wilmer Pickering Hale and Dorr, London
   Panellists
   *Mark Pieth*, University of Basel, Basel
   *Thomas Werlen*, Quinn Emanuel Urquhart & Sullivan, Zurich
   *Michael W. Faske*, EY, Zurich
3. **Panel 2: Impact of Corruption on Substantive Matters**
   The Tribunal's Jurisdiction and the Arbitrability of Issues of Corruption.
   The Impact of Corruption on the Contract, including the Issue of Applicable Law
   Investment Arbitration specific Issues
   Moderator
   *Mariella Orelli*, Homburger, Zurich
   Panellists
   *Niklaus Pitkowitz*, Graf & Pitkowitz Rechtsanwälte, Wien
   *Christoph Müller*, University of Neuchâtel, Neuchâtel
   *Andrea Menaker*, White & Case, London
4. **Panel 3: The Impact of Alleged or Demonstrated Corruption on the Arbitral Process**
   If Corruption Taints the Process itself: Corrupt Arbitrators, Experts and Witnesses
   Duty and Power of Arbitrators to Investigate and Evidentiary Issues
   Judicial Scrutiny of Corruption-Tainted Arbitral Awards at the Setting Aside and Enforcement Stage

Moderator
*Rikard Wikström-Hermansen*, Roschier, Stockholm
Panellists
*Kate Davies*, Allen & Overy, London
*Pierre Mayer*, Pierre Mayer, Paris
*Anne-Catherine Hahn*, IPrime Legal, Zurich

5. **Panel 4: Role of International Arbitration in Fighting Corruption**
   Duty to Report Suspicion?
   Risk for Personal Liability (Aiding and Abetting)?
   Duty or Right of Arbitrators to Report Suspicion of Corruption to Authorities?
   Is There a Need for Further Action and Initiatives by the Arbitration Community?
   Moderator
   *Ulrike Gantenberg*, Heuking Kühn Lüer Wojtek, Düsseldorf
   Panellists
   *Mark Pieth*, University of Basel, Basel
   *Koh Swee Yen*, WongPartnership, Singapore
   *Stephan Wilske*, Gleiss Lutz, Stuttgart

# Editors

**Andrea Meier** practises arbitration and litigation and is recognised as a leader in her field. She has acted as arbitration counsel or arbitrator in more than eighty arbitrations under various national laws and arbitration rules (ICC, SCAI, DIS, VIAC, WIPO, UNCITRAL, CAS, ad hoc, etc.). A particular focus of Andrea Meier's work is the construction sector. Recent cases also include post-M&A and joint venture disputes and disputes in the pharmaceutical and mobility sectors. Moreover, Andrea Meier regularly represents clients from the financial industry before state courts and arbitral tribunals and advises them on cross-border matters regarding foreign court proceedings (banking secrecy, Article 271 Swiss Criminal Code). She has extensive experience handling a wide array of disputes between banks and customers, banks and service providers and inter-bank disputes. *Chambers Global, Chambers Europe and Who's Who Legal* recognise Andrea Meier as a global arbitration leader. She holds leading functions in key professional organisations. She is a Vice President of ASA (Swiss Arbitration Association) and a member of ASA's Executive Committee, a former ASA below 40 co-chair, a member of the Arbitration Court of SCAI (Swiss Chambers' Arbitration Institution), a member of SCAI's Special Committee, and an arbitrator of the CAS (Court of Arbitration for Sport). She regularly publishes in the field of international arbitration and is a frequent speaker at international arbitration conferences in Switzerland and abroad. Andrea Meier joined Walder Wyss as a partner in 2020. Previously, she was a partner in a renowned boutique law firm for dispute resolution and, from 2003 to 2010, an associate and senior associate in a leading major law firm. Andrea Meier holds a degree in Law and a doctorate degree from the University of Zurich (lic. iur. 1999, Dr. iur. 2007) and an LLM from Harvard Law School (2005).

**Christian Oetiker** is a Partner in VISCHER and a proven specialist in litigation and arbitration. He represents businesses in proceedings before national courts throughout Switzerland as well as before national and foreign arbitral tribunals. He also acts as an arbitrator. Christian studied at the University of St. Gallen (HSG) and the London School of Economics; he has an in-depth understanding of economic issues. He regularly represents both national and international companies from the chemical industry and aviation industry. He also acts as counsel in proceedings on claims based on derivative agreements, which are governed by the ISDA Master Agreement. In addition to dispute resolution, he advises on private international law and unfair competition law. Christian publishes and regularly speaks on litigation and arbitration matters as well as other selected topics. He is a member of the Board of the Swiss Arbitration Association (ASA) and of the Swiss Commission of Arbitration and ADR of the ICC. From 2008 until 2019, he was a member of the Arbitration Court of the Swiss Chambers' Arbitration Institution.

# Contributors

**Kate Davies** is a Partner in Allen & Overy's International Arbitration Group and has extensive expertise in both international commercial and investment treaty arbitration. In relation to her commercial arbitration expertise, Kate has experience of both institutional (e.g., LCIA, ICC, PCA, VIAC, SIAC, ICSID) and ad hoc arbitrations sited in common and civil law jurisdictions. She has expertise in commercial disputes across a range of different industries (including the energy, telecommunications, automotive, technology, construction and pharmaceutical sectors) and arising out of a number of bespoke and industry-specific agreements, including joint venture, shareholder, licensing, distribution, technology transfer, patent and construction agreements. Kate is described as 'phenomenally bright, extremely hardworking, and thoroughly personable' by Legal 500 (UK 2017, International Arbitration). Chambers & Partners recognised Kate as a 'Star Associate' for two years running, before promoting her to its main rankings in 2015, where clients and peers have described her as is 'very helpful, very knowledgeable', 'excellent', 'truly brilliant', 'very sensible and highly pragmatic' and a '"really talented" advocate'. In Chambers UK 2016, she was 'tipped as a "leader of the future" by commentators, who praise her significant advocacy skills'. Kate is ranked as a specialist in *Who's Who Legal*: Arbitration 2019. *Who's Who Legal*: Arbitration – Future Leaders 2017 reported that Kate is a 'very talented young lawyer', 'one of the foremost experts in this field' and 'extremely focused, driven and hardworking with enormous energy'.

**Michael W. Faske** is head of EY's Forensic & Integrity Services Group in Switzerland. Altogether, Michael has close to twenty years of relevant work experience in fraud and investigations, financial and economic damage, anti-money laundering investigations, fraud prevention, compliance matter issues as well as in corporate legal issues. Additionally, Michael is a guest lecturer at the Lucerne University of Applied Science and Arts in the Competence Centre for Forensic and Economic Crime, as well as at the ESMT (European School of Management and Technology). He is also the author of various Thought Leadership on the topic of economic crime and corporate compliance.

**Ulrike Gantenberg** is the founder of Gantenberg Dispute Experts and highly recognized in the field of dispute resolution – in particular for national and international arbitration. She acts as counsel and arbitrator (chair, sole and co-arbitrator) in complex litigation and international arbitration proceedings (ad hoc, DIS, ICC, LCIA, VIAC, SCC etc.), particularly in post-M&A, corporate/licence, construction and investor-state disputes, and as counsel in DAB proceedings regarding turnkey and energy projects. As a qualified German lawyer with experience working in France, Ulrike Gantenberg is particularly dedicated to international work due to her international clients and her global network. Besides German, she speaks English and French fluently. Her vast experience as an arbitrator impacts her quality of counsel work. Ulrike combines technical expertise with strategic advice to pursue or defend claims on behalf of her clients. For more than ten years, she has also advised on mergers, restructuring and inter-group (re-)structuring. She frequently speaks and publishes on issues of international arbitration and international private law.

**Koh Swee Yen** is a partner in the commercial and corporate disputes and international arbitration practices at WongPartnership LLP. Ms Koh is the vice-chair of the IBA Arbitration Committee. She is also the vice-chair of the IPBA Dispute Resolution and Arbitration Committee and a member of the editorial board of the ICC Dispute Resolution Bulletin and the ICCA-ASIL Task Force on Damages. Ms Koh is recommended as a leading practitioner in various legal publications, including *The Legal 500*, *Chambers Global* and *Benchmark Litigation Asia-Pacific*. Most recently, she has been listed as one of the world's leading arbitration practitioners in *Who's Who Legal: Arbitration 2020* and as a recognised expert in *Commercial Arbitration in Experts Guides 2019: The World's Finest Lawyers Chosen By Their Peers*. Described as being *'in a league of her own'*, *'extremely talented'* and *'incredibly hardworking and persistent'* with a *'very deep understanding of the law'* by *Chambers Global*, sources also praise her for a *'keen sense of strategy'* and *'great ability to quickly grasp her clients' perspective and understand their commercial issues'*. *The Legal 500* says that Swee Yen is the *'go-to disputes lawyer in Singapore'*, with an *'ability to zone right in on the issues with precision and confidence'*, and is *'brilliant, decisive and fearless'*.

**Anne-Catherine Hahn** is a partner with IPrime Legal, a boutique firm in Zurich focusing on technology and technology disputes. Relying on many years of experience as a partner with Baker McKenzie, where she was a member of the firm's steering committee for the EMEA dispute resolution practice group, Anne-Catherine Hahn today acts as counsel, arbitrator and mediator in commercial disputes. Many of her cases are situated at the crossroads of civil, regulatory and criminal law, and most relate to the technology and life sciences sector. Ms Hahn holds a bilingual degree in Law ('MA') and a PhD from the University of Fribourg (Walter Hug Foundation Prize; Peter Jäggi Foundation Prize), as well as an LLM from the University of Michigan. She has for many years taught courses at the University of Fribourg in Switzerland, was a visiting researcher at the National University of Singapore, and regularly publishes on her areas of practice. *WWL* recognises Anne-Catherine Hahn as a 'Future Leader' and commends her as an 'excellent litigator' with 'deep expertise in civil, commercial and criminal disputes', while *Legal 500* recommended her as a 'stand-out litigator'. As a trained mediator, she also acts as President of a conciliation commission in charge of gender equality issues within the ETH Domain, a Swiss network of high-profile technical universities and research institutions.

**Pierre Mayer** Internationally recognised for his competence, extensive experience and intellectual honesty, Professor Pierre Mayer is considered one of the few great names of international arbitration. He now acts mainly as an arbitrator in both commercial and investment arbitration procedures. He is a specialist in international arbitration law and private international law, two subjects which he has taught for decades at the University of Paris I (Panthéon-Sorbonne), where he was a professor from 1984 to 2012 and has been an emeritus professor since 2012. Prior to setting up his own office, Professor Pierre Mayer practised with Coudert Brothers, Clifford Chance and Dechert, where he was a partner for ten years. A qualified French *avocat*, Professor Pierre Mayer has acted as counsel or arbitrator in hundreds of proceedings under a variety of ad hoc or institutional arbitration rules in commercial and investment matters. His experience spans a variety of sectors and all forms of contracts. Professor Pierre Mayer regularly speaks at conferences. He is the author of the reference textbook on French international private law and of a general course at the Hague Academy of International Law. He has published dozens of articles on arbitration law and practice and on private international law. He is also, *inter alia*, former president of the International Academy for Arbitration Law, member of the council of the ICC Institute of World Business Law, member of the board of the *Comité français de l'arbitrage*, member of the *Institut de droit international*, and former President of the committee on international commercial arbitration of the International Law Association. A French national, Professor Pierre Mayer is fluent in English. *WWL* says: *Pierre Mayer is 'one of the most sophisticated and intelligent arbitrators in the market' according to peers who 'have a lot of respect for his work' as both arbitrator and counsel.*

**Andrea Menaker** has focused her career exclusively on investment arbitration for the past twenty years. After more than ten years practising as a partner in White & Case's Washington DC office, where she has represented respondent States and claimant investors in equal measure in some of the most groundbreaking investment arbitration cases, Andrea recently transferred to London to grow the Firm's investment arbitration treaty practice there. Before joining White & Case, Andrea was Chief of the NAFTA Arbitration Division for the US Department of State, where she was lead counsel for the US in NAFTA Chapter Eleven arbitrations. Andrea is a Board Member of the Arbitration Institute of the Stockholm Chamber of Commerce (SCC), a Council Member of the Hong Kong International Arbitration Centre (HKIAC), a Board Member of the Association Suisse de l'Arbitrage (ASA), a past Chair of the Programme Committee for ICCA's Congress in Mauritius, a past Executive Council Member for the American Society of International Law (ASIL), and a former adjunct professor at Georgetown University Law Centre, where she taught international arbitration. Andrea frequently speaks and publishes on investment arbitration issues.

**Professor Christoph Müller** is a professor at the University of Neuchâtel (Switzerland) teaching contract law, tort law, comparative private law and contract drafting. From 2014 to 2016, he was the dean of the faculty of law. He is also a life member of Clare Hall College (Cambridge, UK). Over the last twenty-five years, Christoph has acted as (presiding, sole and co-) arbitrator, legal expert and counsel in more than 150 international commercial arbitrations. He is familiar with various substantive laws (in particular Swiss, English, US, German and French) and both institutional (ICC, Swiss Rules, LCIA, DIS, WIPO, TAS) and ad hoc arbitration. His main fields of arbitral practice are distribution, corporate law, finance and banking, JV, consortia and shareholder agreements and sale and purchase agreements. Christoph is a member of the SCAI Arbitration Court (including its special committee), an ASA executive committee and board member and a CIArb fellow. He is a head lecturer of the Swiss Arbitration Academy and the CAS in arbitration at the Universities of Neuchâtel and Lucerne. He also is an arbitrator on the general list of the Court of Arbitration for Sport (CAS). Christoph is the author of numerous books and articles in the fields of international arbitration, contract law, tort law and comparative private law. His next book, *Swiss Contract Law in International Commercial Arbitration*, will be published by Cambridge University Press. Christoph was admitted to the Swiss Bar in 1997. He holds an LLM (Columbia Law School) and a juris doctor degree (University of Neuchâtel). In 2016-2017, Christoph was a visiting scholar at the University of Cambridge (UK).

**Mariella Orelli** is a partner in Homburger's litigation and arbitration team. She has acted as party counsel in contentious matters before international arbitral tribunals in Switzerland and abroad as well as before state courts, including the Zurich Commercial Court and administrative courts. She has acted as counsel in various landmark cases, such as the first-ever successful application for the revision of an arbitral award and the first decision by the Swiss Supreme Court on recognition and enforcement of *Mareva* injunctions in Switzerland. Mariella has also acted as an arbitrator, both as a chairwoman and as a party-appointed arbitrator. She also represents clients in investment arbitration matters. She is familiar with a number of industries, including financial markets, pharma, energy and construction, and a wide range of M&A disputes. Her advisory practice also includes assisting clients in regulatory matters in the energy sector. Mariella is a member of the Zurich and Swiss Bar Associations, the IBA, the Swiss Arbitration Association and other professional associations. She is a co-author of *Commentary on Swiss Federal Act on Jurisdiction and Enforcement* and *Practitioners' Guide to Arbitration in Switzerland*. She has also published various articles. She is fluent in Italian, German, English and French. Between 1993 and 1998, Mariella served as a clerk with the District Court in Zurich and the Commercial Court of the Canton of Zurich. After graduating from the University of Zurich (1992), she was admitted to the Bar (1996) and obtained her LLM from the College of Europe (1999). In 2000, she was a foreign associate at Herbert Smith in London (dispute resolution).

**Professor Mark Pieth** is a Professor of Criminal Law at Basel University since 1993. In particular, in his other professional activities as an international and national regulator, as a legal expert, defence lawyer and judge, as well as a compliance monitor and compliance advisor, he has been confronted with political and economic aspects of power management, including with all forms of abuse of power. One of his key ambitions, both in public and the private domain, has been to develop methods to challenge such abuses (in an international setting with the help of regulation and country monitoring, in the private sector by enforcing compliance standards and through advocacy as well as litigation, in particular in the area of arbitration). The research and policy institute he founded at the University of Basel, the Basel Institute on Governance is one of the key tools to reach these goals.

**Nikolaus Pitkowitz** is the founding partner of Graf & Pitkowitz and head of the firm's dispute resolution and real estate practice groups. He has been practising law since 1985; his practice, which has always been very international with a strong focus on CEE, was initially mainly comprised of transactional work in the fields of real estate and M&A and quickly expanded to international dispute resolution. Nikolaus is considered one of the foremost Austrian dispute resolution practitioners. He acted as counsel and arbitrator in a multitude of international arbitrations, including several high-profile disputes, most notably as counsel in the largest pending Austrian arbitration (a multibillion telecom dispute). Nikolaus is also active as counsel in significant real estate projects and currently serves as chair of the IBA Real Estate Section, the world's largest association of real estate practitioners.

**Professor Dr Maxi Scherer** is a Professor of Law at the Queen Mary University of London, School of International Arbitration, where she holds the Chair for International Arbitration, Dispute Resolution and Energy Law. She is also a Special Counsel at Wilmer Cutler Pickering Hale and Dorr LLP in London admitted to the Bar in Paris (France) and as a solicitor (England and Wales). Maxi has extensive experience with arbitral practice both in civil and common law systems, with a particular focus on the energy sector. She has represented clients, provided expert opinions and sat as arbitrator in more than 100 commercial and investor-state arbitrations (ad hoc and DIS, HKIAC, ICC, ICSID, LCIA, PCA, SCC, etc.) under a broad variety of governing laws and seats. She has been regularly ranked by *Who's Who Legal, The Legal 500*, etc., as a leading arbitration practitioner: she was identified repeatedly amongst the top 20 'Global Elite Thought Leaders'. Maxi publishes extensively in the field of international arbitration, including International Arbitration in the Energy Sector (OUP, 2018). She is the General Editor of the Kluwer Journal of International Arbitration. She holds many other public appointments and commissions of trust including being a member of the panel of arbitrators (ICSID); a Vice-President of the London Court of International Arbitration (LCIA); a member of the International Advisory Board of the Vienna International Arbitral Centre (VIAC) and Drafting Committee for new protocols to the Arbitration Rules of the Permanent Court of Arbitration (PCA).

**Thomas Werlen** is the Managing Partner of Quinn Emanuel Urquhart & Sullivan (Schweiz) GmbH. Thomas is recognised as one of the top attorneys in Switzerland, reflecting his unique experience in law firms in New York and London. He has been involved as lead counsel in some of the highest-profile civil and criminal matters in Switzerland. Prior to joining Quinn Emanuel, Thomas served as Group General Counsel and a member of the Executive Committee for Novartis. Before joining Novartis in 2006, Thomas was a Partner at Allen & Overy in London, covering US-related derivatives, capital markets and M&A transactions for European-based clients. Prior to that, he was associated with Cravath, Swaine & Moore and Davis Polk & Wardwell in New York and London, respectively. Thomas's practice focuses on white-collar cases and corporate investigations as well as on complex litigation and arbitration, often involving multiple jurisdictions.

**Rikard Wikström-Hermansen** is a Stockholm-based Partner at Roschier focusing on Swedish and international commercial arbitration as well as Swedish court proceedings. He was appointed Lawyer of the Year for Sweden by *Benchmark Litigation* in both 2019 and 2020. Rikard has represented Swedish, foreign and multinational corporations before courts and arbitral tribunals under various arbitration rules such as the SCC, the ICC, the SIAC and the UNCITRAL rules. The disputes have involved many different business sectors, such as oil & gas, construction, the automotive industry and M&A disputes. Rikard also regularly sits as an arbitrator and has chaired several international commercial arbitrations – governed by English, Swedish and Russian law – involving Danish, Egyptian, Estonian, German, Norwegian, Russian, Spanish and Swedish parties.

**Dr Stephan Wilske, LLM**, is a partner in the Gleiss Lutz Dispute Resolution Practice Group and regularly advises clients in international commercial and investment arbitration proceedings, as well as in cross-border litigation. He regularly serves as arbitrator (party-appointed or chair) in international arbitrations. He is admitted in New York (1997), Germany (1997), and to the US Court of Appeals for the Federal Circuit (2007), the US Supreme Court (2009) and the US Court of Appeals for the Second Circuit (2010). Stephan is a Fellow of the Chartered Institute of Arbitrators (FCIArb) and of the Asian Institute of Alternative Dispute Resolution, as well as a member of the American Law Institute (ALI). He is International Advisor to the Korean Institute of Technology and the Law (KITAL), a member of the SIAC Users', Senior Committee Member of the Contemporary Asia Arbitration Journal, Kluwer ITA Country Law Reporter for Turkey (together with Ismail Esin), member of the Editorial Board of ARBITRATION – The International Journal of Arbitration, Mediation and Dispute Management, Advisory Committee Member of the Swiss Arbitration Academy (SAA) and a contributor to the Max Planck Encyclopedia of Public International Law (MPEPIL). Since 2019, he is a Vice-President of the CAAI Court of Arbitration. He teaches at various German universities, including the Universities of Heidelberg and Jena. In 2010, Stephan was a visiting professor at the National Taiwan University College of Law. Stephan Wilske has studied at the Université d'Aix-Marseille III (Maîtrise en Droit, 1987), University of Tübingen (First State Exam, 1990; MA in Political Sciences, 1991; Dr iur. 1998) and The University of Chicago Law School (LLM; Casper Platt Award 1996).

# Table of Contents

# Preface

This volume of the ASA Special Series reproduces the transcribed presentations and lively discussions at the ASA Annual Full Day Conference of 1 February 2019 held in Geneva on the topic 'Arbitration and Corruption'.

The first panel moderated by Prof. Maxi Scherer set out many facets of corruption and the causes that come with it. Prof. Mark Pieth set out the legal framework of corruption, in particular the aspects of criminal law. Michael W. Faske showed the cost of corruption from an economic perspective. Thomas Werlen gave practical tips for identifying suspicious relationships.

What law do I need to apply? Who needs to establish that my suspicion of corruption was right or wrong? How should I bring this issue before the parties? What would be the impact on the agency agreement, and what law is relevant for this question?

Panels 2 and 3 gave answers to these questions. The second panel, moderated by Mariella Orelli, dealt with the impact of corruption on substantive matters. Andrea Menaker gave an insight into the question of jurisdiction and the arbitrability of issues of corruption and explained the aspects of corruption that are specific to investment arbitration. Prof. Christoph Müller reviewed the impact of corruption on the contracts, including the law that has to be applied to these questions. Nikolaus Pitkowitz explained what strategic considerations one has to make when confronted with a corruption-tainted contract.

The third panel, moderated by Rikard Wikström-Hermansen, put the focus on the arbitral process and the question of what impact issues of corruption have. Kate Davies examined what happens if corruption taints the process itself, in particular in the case of corrupt arbitrators, experts and witnesses. Pierre Mayer discussed the duty and the power of arbitrators to investigate corruption and the related evidentiary issues. Anne-Catherine Hahn spoke about the judicial scrutiny of corruption-tainted arbitral awards at the setting aside and enforcement stage.

The fourth panel, led by Ulrike Gantenberg, investigated the role of arbitration in fighting corruption and whether there is any such role. Prof. Mark Pieth examined from a criminal law point of view whether there is a duty to report suspicion of corruption and the related risk of personal liability. Kow Swee Yen investigated the duty to report a suspicion of corruption to authorities. Stephan Wilske considered the questions of whether there is a need for further action and initiatives by the arbitration community.

On behalf of the ASA Swiss Arbitration Association, we would like to thank the moderators and panellists for all the time and effort they have dedicated to the success of the Conference. It was a great pleasure to organise and lead this Conference with such a great number of excellent and distinguished arbitration practitioners.

Our special thanks and gratitude goes to former ASA Executive Director, Alex McLin, and his Assistant, Songea Dehne, for the perfect handling of all organisational and administrative matters relating to the Conference and to Robyn Nott for her impeccable transcription services.

We hope that all those who could make it to Geneva on 1 February 2019 enjoyed the various contributions and debates as much as we did. Moreover, we hope that this volume of the ASA Special Series provides both interesting and entertaining reading, not only to the participants but also to all those who would have wished to attend.

Between the conference in February 2019 and today, the world has been hit by COVID-19. As a consequence, most events, at which the arbitration community would gather as it did in February 2019 in Geneva, were cancelled. We sincerely hope that it will soon be possible again to meet in person to exchange views on relevant topics. We look forward to it.

*Andrea Meier / Christian Oetiker*
*Zurich / Basel, Autumn of 2020*

# Welcome Address and Introduction to the Conference Topic

*Andrea Meier & Christian Oetiker*

**ANDREA MEIER:**

Welcome everybody, and thank you for coming to Geneva. Our today's conference deals with arbitration and corruption. We all know what arbitration is, but we were wondering do we really know what we mean when we use the word corruption.

Corruption is probably as old as mankind. No country, empire, regime or private sector has ever been exempt, not even the home of Western philosophy, Ancient Greece. An ancient Greek family, the Alcmaeonidae, are said to have bribed the Oracle at Delphi to persuade Sparta to free Athens. Since the Oracle spoke for the God Apollo, this was considered proof that even the Gods could be bribed.

The Romans did not do much better. In fact, they brought bribery to a whole new level. Julius Caesar won his consulship through massive electoral bribery. He was not alone; bribery was rampant. Each group and party tried to manipulate the elections for its own interest. In fact, historians consider that corruption was the main reason for the downfall of the Roman Republic and the rise of the despots.

Corruption is an old phenomenon, but the sensibility towards corruption has grown over the past twenty years. There is increasing regulatory scrutiny, and there is the rise of global anti-corruption law.

The phenomenon of corruption by far exceeds the area of law. It is dealt with by many different disciplines such as philosophy, sociology, psychology and economics. They all try to understand what makes humans engage in corrupt behaviour, what the costs are, and how we can discourage it.

When is it that we cross these ethical boundaries that make bad behaviour an act of corruption? How to know if one is corrupt? I came across a discussion forum on the Web, and most people struggle with a clear answer, but one person came up with this simple rule: you know you are corrupt if you take more food because someone else will pay the bill.

Sociology tells us it is a bit more complex than that. Sociologists say that corruption requires an exchange relationship. It also requires that the party acts as a representative of third parties and that it violates norms designed to protect the third parties and for private gain.

Then there is anthropology.

Anthropologists say that we cannot disregard a specific cultural context and value system when studying corruption. We should see corruption not as an isolated act but within a web of social relations, and they point out the difficulty to distinguish between gift and bribe in certain societies.

Psychology tells us about the motivations of people to adapt corrupt behaviour. Psychologists found that individuals holding power are more likely to act corruptly. Corrupt behaviour is also more likely when individuals stand to gain personally, have lower self-control, perceive that corruption may only cause indirect harm, and when they work in organisations that do not punish unethical behaviour.

Finally, economics tells us about the costs of corruption. The costs are massive.

Corruption is one of the main obstacles to sustainable development of a society and has a significant negative impact on a country's productivity. It particularly punishes the poor because they cannot afford to pay bribes to access basic services, such as health care or education.

The many facets of corruption and the causes that come with it will be addressed by our first panel. We will learn about the legal framework of corruption and its cost from an economic perspective, and we will get practical tips for identifying suspicious relationships.

This will set the ground for our later panels.

Since arbitration operates on a global level, it cannot surprise us that corruption has reached arbitration as well. If an arbitrator indeed has reason to suspect that corruption is involved in his or her arbitration, the problems are just about to start.

**CHRISTIAN OETIKER:**

On 24 May 2018, the ICC Court appointed me as Sole Arbitrator in a case. The dispute was between a claimant from 'Offshoria' and a respondent from the Middle East. It concerned claims out of an agency agreement.

The case management conference took place on 6 June 2018, and the Terms of Reference were signed on the same day. Respondent had requested a stay of the proceedings from the outset in Answer to the Request for Arbitration, and after having heard the parties, I rejected that motion.

The claimant submitted the Statement of Claim on 3 September 2018. By that time, I had received the Request for Arbitration, the Answer and Statement of Claim. One issue caught my attention. The main exponent, or maybe the sole exponent, of the claimant, who was the respondent's agent, was at the same time the head of the procurement department of a customer of the respondent, and it had been the claimant who had introduced that customer to the respondent.

Based on the literature on arbitration and corruption, I identified a number of red flags that were present in this case. First, the issue related to a sector prone to corruption, namely defence; second, the agency agreement in the dispute related to the main contract between the respondent and the customer of the respondent; third, an officer of that customer was an officer of the agent; fourth, there was only a little time lag between the execution of the agency agreement and the conclusion of the main contract; fifth, activities of the agent were not clearly defined in the consulting agreement; sixth, although the agent was based in 'Offshoria', the fees had to be paid into another country, namely Liechtenstein; seventh, there was no website or publicly available information on the agent; eighth, at this stage, there was no evidence whatsoever for any activity of the agent.

On 29 October 2018, the respondent submitted the Statement of Defence. I checked whether the respondent dealt with any of the issues that had caught my attention. However, it did not dispel any of the red flags but rather confirmed some relevant cornerstones.

There I was: happy that I had been appointed by the ICC and now confronted with a situation that raised numerous questions. What should I do with all these red flags? Where could I find an appropriate definition of corruption?

What law did I need to apply? Who needs to establish that my suspicion of corruption was right or wrong? How should I bring this issue before the parties? What would be the impact on the agency agreement, and what law is relevant for this question?

Panels 2 and 3 will give answers to these questions. Panel 2 will deal with the impact of corruption on substantive matters. This includes the question of jurisdiction and the arbitrability of issues of corruption. Panel 2 will also review the impact of corruption on the contracts, including the law that has to be applied to these questions.

Furthermore, it will explain what strategic considerations one has to make when confronted with a corruption-tainted contract. This will include the specific perspectives of the claimant and the respondent. Also, the panel will deal with the aspects of corruption that are specific to investment arbitration.

Panel 3 then puts the focus on the arbitral process and the question of what impact issues of corruption have. It will deal with a number of my questions, in particular, the duty and the power of arbitrators to investigate issues of corruption and the related evidentiary issues.

This panel will explain the impact at the setting aside and enforcement stage.

Finally, the panel will deal with the unfortunate situation that corruption taints the process itself through corrupt arbitrators, experts and witnesses.

**ANDREA MEIER:**

Then we conclude today with panel 4, who will talk about the role of arbitration in fighting corruption or whether there is any such role. We were also hoping actually to hear from Mr Bertossa, the First Prosecutor of the Canton of Geneva, first-hand about the risks that arbitrators face.

Unfortunately, he had to cancel on very short notice for reasons beyond his control, but we are very happy that Professor Pieth, Professor for Criminal Law, agreed to step in. The panel has also had many discussions with Mr Bertossa in preparation for his panel, so they can certainly give you a view on how the prosecutor sees our responsibilities.

We are very much looking forward to the proposals that panel 4 and the audience is going to make on what is the way forward for the arbitration community facing the challenge of corruption.

With that, we conclude our overview. I want to introduce our first moderator for today, Professor Maxi Scherer. She is a special counsel at Wilmer Hale's Litigation/Controversy Department, and she is a member of Wilmer Hale's International Arbitration Practice Group. She is also a distinguished academic, a full-time tenured Professor of Law at the Queen Mary University London, and she is recognised in *Who's Who Legal* arbitration for her strong combination of practice and academia. In my humble opinion, she is simply brilliant, so we are thrilled to have her here today.

**CHRISTIAN OETIKER:**

Two organisational issues. We will publish a book on this conference in the ASA Special Series. For this purpose, Robyn Nott does a transcript of today's conference.

Hence, if you make a question or comment, please clearly state your name. If your question and comment are part of the book, you will have a chance to proofread your contribution before publication. You can also then decide to withdraw your question depending on the answer. You can also make it better. We can also add footnotes to your questions.

Second, we have allotted special time at breaks for networking, but because of this, we kindly ask you to come back on time so that the panels are not delayed.

# Panel 1: Corruption – What Does It Really Mean?

*Moderated by Maxi Scherer*

---

**MAXI SCHERER:**

Thank you to both of you for your kind words of introduction and the invitation to be here this morning. It is always a pleasure to be at the ASA and particularly in Switzerland in Geneva.

The first panel this morning asks the question: corruption – what does it really mean? It seems a simple, maybe even simplistic, question, but, as we all know, simple questions can raise quite complicated and complex underlying issues.

I am, therefore, very much delighted to have three panellists on my side to address this question.

What we are going to do is take certain sub-questions in turn. I will introduce our distinguished panellists in turn, so we have enough time in the end for questions if anyone still wants to ask questions after the introduction.

We are going to first start with our first panellist on my immediate right, Professor Mark Pieth, Professor of Criminal Law at the University of Basel, and his research and scholarship focus on economic crime.

In his prior life, before becoming a Professor at the University of Basel, he held a number of positions. If I were to tell all of them, we would still be here till afternoon, but I wanted to highlight a couple of them that I think are particularly insightful for today's debate.

He has been Head of Section – Economic and Organised Crime at the Swiss Federal Office of Justice. He has chaired the OECD Working Group on Bribery. He was on the committee that oversaw the reform process of FIFA. I definitely wanted to mention that one! He held several positions in the African Development Bank. He has also started an initiative fighting against corruption, so maybe he will tell us more about that.

Mark will set the scene in trying to define what is corruption and what is the legal and regulatory framework for the entire debate today.

# How to Define Corruption?

*Mark Pieth*

**MARK PIETH:**

Ladies and gentlemen, dear colleagues – I trust professors do not use PowerPoints, so you have to make do with what you are getting.

I want to address three issues quite briefly: the challenges related to corruption – some of the topics have already been discussed; then why are we suddenly so interested in this topic; and then, from the perspective of a criminal lawyer, what do I believe is the impact of the topic on arbitration, all that very briefly.

Corruption is really not a new topic; it is an age-old topic. Andrea raised the question of what makes humans engage in corruption. I believe there are maybe two motives, and one is the least problematic: greed is certainly an element, but greed is a situation similar to somebody caught with his hand in the till.

For the second motivation, access to power and maintenance of power is, for me, the more delicate one. It is sufficient to think of, for instance, Idi Amin taking billions out of state coffers in order then to pay off his cronies and stay in power for years. It was quite significant that at the end of his rule, Idi Amin had no money left at all because he had never taken it for himself, in that sense, except to stay in power.

Obviously, we have been looking at what does it do to society. It is very clear, even in Switzerland. I am from the Grisons; I am thinking of Engadine; this is not the classic corruption, but if you manipulate public procurement to the extent that everything is pre-organised, we have a situation close to corruption. What it does to us is we pay simply more than we should be paying, so additional cost.

That is the harmless end of it. If you go down to the global south, it has much more dramatic consequences. I am thinking of a mining company, which I will not name, trying to lower its tax bill by half a billion in Congo. Half a billion to Congo means about the size of the education budget, probably also the health budget. You can choose: no education or no health because one has actually dispensed of that half a billion. In an extreme case, corruption can kill. It is not an exaggeration if one says that.

Both in the north and in the south, corruption undermines trust in public institutions. Again, this may seem weak, but it is fundamental because we need the rule of law. We are absolutely dependent on that; for instance, national courts are reliable.

If you look at the business world, there might be additional points. We do not like to be extorted, and besides for business transnational bribery, bribery of foreign public officials especially is also seen as a form of unfair competition.

The question crops up why would we now be particularly concerned with a topic, with a challenge, that we have been faced for thousands of years? You all know the history of the Foreign Corrupt Practices Act (FCPA), this bit of legislation of the United States of 1977. It is the law that every multinational enterprise fears, and it is what gives you a job. We live off that fear.

One still does not really know, as far as I can judge, why one actually created the Act, people say it was Watergate. Maybe it was the fall-out of Watergate. It was the Tanaka Lockheed scandal and the question: shouldn't the US foreign policy be defined by the state rather than individual companies? Some people are saying one wanted to prevent the defence industry from exporting to Arab nations.

So, you have all sorts of fantastic interpretations as to why this law was created at that time and at that point in time.

My role, as you pointed out, was that of the Chairman of the Organisation for Economic Co-operation and Development (OECD) Working Group on Bribery for twenty-five years. We internationalised the FCPA and basically bullied the forty countries in the Group to enact laws.

The question, of course, poses itself: why was that possible? It did not happen in 1977; it happened from 1997 onwards when the Convention was adopted. Basically, we started working in 1989, and that is no coincidence; it is around the fall of the Berlin wall. It is about globalisation. It is about new markets developing and industries also in Europe or Japan realising that they were going to lose out on the world markets if they left it to the irrationality of some agent who had the better relationship with the President whether they were going to have the 20,000 jobs that were on the line with a concrete case.

I think there was a very solid economic reason why one would in 1989/1990 start with that work. It is no coincidence that exactly at the same moment, also another group I was participating in, the Financial Action Task Force on Money Laundering, took off. It is all that wave of globalisation.

You know that what made things really move was this monitoring process, exposing countries in what is called soft law, but it is not very soft; it is politically a very tough method. Over time several regional treaties, you know them, Council of Europe, European Union, OAS and African Union, a whole series of international treaties were developed, and the development ended with the UNCAC treaty. What you find at the end of the 1990s or early 2000s is a new standard emerging, countries nationally implementing laws and some countries even applying them.

The question is, what does that mean for arbitration? There is an interesting phenomenon. From my vantage point, I would say there is mutual distrust. Arbitration lives off parties preferring a justice system based on their own rules to state justice. They distrust, to some extent, state justice. It is supposed to be quicker – I am not sure.

It is supposed to be cheaper – I am not sure at all – but it is certainly more discreet. Maybe at points, it is actually preferable because the arbitrators are brighter than the national judges. I think we have to be quite politically incorrect!

The other side of the coin is that the international standard-setters, take a person like me or the OECD, are uneasy about the world of arbitration because they believe that is a black box where things happen outside their control, and we are not at all sure whether a new standard is being applied in that world. Frankly, it is true that arbitrators have been hesitant to pick up standards on corruption or money laundering and so on.

If international organisations like the OECD are uneasy, it is about the vast world of major contracts, just think of infrastructure or defence, that elude not only national justice but also those international standards. That is basically where we mutually are looking at each other with distrust. Now the question is: what is happening?

In my view, we are experiencing a time of change, and the fact that you are holding this conference on this topic testifies it, but the challenges remain high. It is quite uncertain, I understand – and we will revisit this issue in the fourth panel – whether arbitrators are there to pursue transnational public policy, as it is said. Also, the relationship of this code word 'transnational public policy' to national laws or laws of choice is still very open, I believe.

Even if you do believe that arbitrators should be listening to parties raising defences of corruption or extortion, then the questions only really start. The evidentiary issues we will be discussing shortly. Then, of course, once you have a finding of corruption, you then have to ask yourself – what now? What do we do with this? Do we refuse jurisdiction? Do we say it is not arbitrable? Do we say it is on merits and we will find ourselves in a balancing exercise?

Then, of course, the big question at the very end: do I have to tell prosecutors? Am I possibly myself, as an arbitrator, criminally liable?

These are some of the issues. Just to finish off, I had in the last fifteen years continuously been confronted with questions in the role of the expert. I had the impression that every tribunal reinvents the wheel. Everybody starts at zero and develops new procedural rules and the whole catalogue of topics that you are discussing today. It would be good to have some kind of tool kit.

We, in Basel, started playing around with a paper suggesting to arbitrators what they could do if they are confronted with such a topic. The idea is not to tell them: this is what you need to do. It is not about prescription or prescriptive language but just to offer a sort of guidance on what could be done instead of having to start from scratch every time.

I will stop here, and we will have a chance to discuss.

**MAXI SCHERER:**

Thank you, Mark. Before I give the floor to the other panellists to comment, if I may, it is a little bit off-the-cuff question; we did not prepare this, so you are more than welcome to decline. When I heard you develop the historical framework of the different legal instruments and your insight, I would like to ask you what is, in your view, the scheme for the next steps? How do we go from here in the next couple of years in terms of the overall regulatory framework?

**MARK PIETH:**

The committee that I left in 2014, of course, plods on, and their major topic is to make things really work. I had mentioned that there is a very patchy, uneven implementation of national laws on corruption. Some states are overactive, like the US, especially when it comes to non-American companies - that is the perception that people get - and others are just doing nothing. Half of the OECD is simply inactive.

From an international perspective with these international bodies, they are trying to twist people's arms and make things really happen. They are not very dynamic in context, so do not expect new moves in contents. What they are trying to do is to expand across the world to get India and China, maybe Indonesia, more excited about this. That is looking at it purely from the international public arena.

The question is, what do we do in the arbitration world? What is to be expected that is more for you?

**MAXI SCHERER:**

That is not necessarily for our panel because our panel is setting the scene for the discussion in the subsequent panels that focus more specifically on arbitration.

**THOMAS WERLEN:**

I am very keen, on the one hand, not to take away the story of my subsequent presentation, but I was very keen, nevertheless, to hear from you, Mark, in a way the answer to what I call a paradox: that at least since 1989, as you said, there has been a lot more done across the world in OECD Anti Bribery and the FCPA in many jurisdictions to rein in corruption and we are still seeing that we are not moving anywhere in that sense.

If you look at the most recent Transparency International corruption index, it seems to be all-in to stay where it was like twenty years ago. That is the major crux that we see and also something that I conduct with a few slides in a minute.

What is your main take, if that is possible? It does not really work, or does it?

**MICHAEL FASKE:**

From a practitioner's view, rather a comment than a question. What we see in the globalised economy is that you see a lot of countries where big corporates are doing business, and they have their individual legislation. In many countries, you have a Corporate Act where you have corporate defence clauses, et cetera. The biggest challenge from a company's side is level playing field problems.

I recall a case from the early 2000s in Switzerland, Panalpina, for example, who got involved in a major FCPA investigation, and the consequence was they had to withdraw from Nigeria because they figured out they could not legally conduct business in Nigeria. Guess what: Nigeria did not become better just because Panalpina pulled out, and some other Asian transport companies picked up the business. Sometimes, companies are complaining, and there are a lot of global initiatives, there is the OECD, but there is still no level playing field according to which companies can orientate, build up a preventive system and organise the governance and compliances.

**MARK PIETH:**

Very briefly on those two points, starting with the second point, it is true the ambition from an international perspective is about creating a level playing field. That was the motive to move; it was about unfair competition. Therefore, what was interesting is the experience when we were monitoring. We never had a situation where one country helped out another country. There is no mutual back-scratching. The Irish would not help the British even though they had, at that time, the same law because they were in competition with each other.

That is very, very strong and very present, but you are right; one is not where one should be on levelling the playing field.

The role of the Non-Governmental Organizations (NGOs) is an interesting one. They came in quite early in this process. TI, Transparency International, was found around 1994, and we started work in 1989, but up to 1994, we did not do very much. We were asking ourselves what would we do if we did something.

At the same time, the Clinton Administration came in and said, 'For God's sake, do something now.' At the same time, Transparency International starting pushing. Since then, it was a kind of to and fro ping pong game with NGOs.

They have a lot of impact in those international fora, as you know. I think you are going to project their chart with the bribe perception index. They have really changed business life quite a bit.

# The Costs of Corruption and How to Fight It

*Thomas Werlen*

**MAXI SCHERER:**

That is a very nice transition to our next subtopic and the slides we will see. The next subtopic is looking at what are the costs of corruption. What are the costs impact on the market but also more globally on society as a whole, and are there economic possibility incentives on how to fight corruption? Thomas Werlen will present this topic.

He is the managing partner of Quinn Emanuel in Zurich. More particularly, he is qualified in New York and Switzerland, and his practice focuses on white-collar crime and complex civil disputes. I will be told off if I mention FIFA again, but he did represent FIFA in criminal investigations here in Switzerland and in the US, as you are all probably aware of.

Interestingly, before joining Quinn Emanuel, he was a group general counsel at Novartis. While I hope you did not have specific knowledge about corruption at the time I think prevention of corruption and, more specifically, or more concretely, the cost of corruption was on your mind.

**THOMAS WERLEN:**

Good morning everyone.

When I was told to come with slides, my dear friend Philipp Habegger said, 'You do not need to bring slides to us here; you should just speak up.' I said we white-collar lawyers charge by the hour, so probably that is why. We will see whether I can tackle the challenge now before a group of arbitrators. Thank you for having me.

We are going to look at the question of the costs of corruption, of why corruption happens, but I wanted to again lay out first what we have seen over the last twenty years, in particular. It actually leads us to the question of why is not more happening to prevent corruption and hopefully also how can we all, and how can you all, contribute, going forward, in the arbitration world to fight corruption.

We have seen clearly now that corruption is perceived as something negative. We have also seen in the last twenty, or thirty years so many initiatives, be it, in particular, the one by Mark Pieth on the OECD side, be it Group of States against Corruption (GRECO), be it NGOs like Transparency International, that have shown how and why corruption has a negative impact on the business overall. These initiatives have actually led to changes in laws throughout the world. As we said before, it was not just the FCPA. We have seen in the period from 2000 to 2010 a number of countries in Europe coming up with new and tough laws, also we have seen in the last ten years China coming forward targeting not only corruption with public officials but also private bribery, so a lot has happened.

Again, with my former corporate hat on, I can tell you that all the large corporations actually, forced or otherwise, want to work on their compliance efforts. There is a lot out there, and even more happening as we speak, to basically come to what we call performance with integrity.

Yet today, with the most recent Transparency International chart - it was a time just for this week actually - you see this world chart [Slide showing countries' Corruption Perceptions Index scores for the year 2018, using a colour-coded world map. Countries with a high perceived corruption level show dark red while countries with a low perceived corruption level show in a light yellow]. It is based on perceived corruption in the public area. I want to flag that. It is difficult to measure it ultimately.

You see, there are red spots like Venezuela, Syria, Libya, so failed states in some sense where it is particularly prevalent. You can see though that a large part of the world is viewed as basically subject to corruption.

If we look at the countries, it is particularly perceived to be prevalent in emerging markets, but it is also interesting if you look at the Transparency International report; more recently, some countries move up some move down. Apparently, this time around, the US moved down a bit as well.

It is prevalent and brings me to this corruption paradox. How can it be that everybody hates it and nevertheless it is here to stay, and it is here to stay notwithstanding it being increasingly illegal but also immoral?

One point and one approach I wanted to bring to your attention today and used the same way in capital markets law, is the disclosure philosophy that should bring at least a rational individual to prevent corruption. If we can bring out the costs and in particular the hidden costs of corruption, people should realise this is bad in the long term.

What one has to challenge in the following working hypothesis: If we pay bribes, we will get more business. If I receive bribes, I will directly get a benefit, so short-term corruption is something that seems to be an upside. What one needs to take into account, is what happens if this corruption is not going to work out because eventually, it will come out.

For instance, we see individuals that sometimes, like in the FIFA case, get the money *themselves* and hurt the company that they deprive of that money, e.g. FIFA. Others, e.g. people that work at companies like Siemens, bribe because they want to get more business for *their company*, so their bonus gets higher. One way or another, these people would probably not at that moment take into account the cost that corruption entails both for them personally (e.g. jail) and for their company (that will obviously have to pay fines and other costs that are significant).

Second, and probably even more importantly - and Mark, you mentioned it - with respect to some situations in Congo, the hidden costs of corruption are actually even much worse. So: short-term benefit, long-term downside, but if we tell people about it, they should realise it, and that is what I want to do right now.

You see in the example of Siemens; this is now an FCPA case; ten years ago, in Germany, led to massive fines, led also to individuals being chased all over the world. If you look at the bottom line, you will see the costs of such fines in a number of jurisdictions, Europe, the US, both SEC and the DOJ. You also see the legal, and I have to say also accounting firm, fees that were run-up in order to defend this case, incredible. You also see, and interestingly cheaper, to subsequent compliance measures, hiring a lot of compliance staff to fight it.

That is a staggering number, I think, but you will also see that there is throughout, in the last ten years, an increasing set of enforcement.

Mark is right; if you look at this list, it is more non-US companies than US companies that you see [Slide showing the current top ten US FCPA enforcement actions of all time based on penalties and disgorgement (in USD)]. You also see that the numbers have gone up. If you look at the years, there is quite a lot of activity in the last few years, in particular.

More importantly, though, apart from these direct costs that are apparent to everyone, there is an additional hidden cost of corruption. The Brazil situation in the last few years is a case on point. Starting with 'Lava Jato' and Odebrecht and continuing with Petrobras, corruption brought this country to get rid of the old leaders and bring a new leader, Bolsonaro, on the anti-corruption platform.

The impact of corrupt regimes, of corruption all-in, can also be seen in Venezuela, a country that has oil like no other in the world, more than in the Gulf, has been brought down by a group of people taking control of the oil industry, PDVSA, and once again, as we speak, involved in white-collar investigations in this particular situation throughout the world.

The bottom line for me is, it is pretty clear that while it is difficult to measure these costs, it is significant. Notwithstanding that, I want to not take away the number that the World Bank is bringing about. They say it is USD 2.6 trillion a year, so 2,600 billion, which is about 5% of the global economy that may be affected. It is obviously difficult to measure in some sense.

When you work in a large company, you know that people are set targets. They need in their particular country to bring in certain revenue every year. The incentive when you are not selling enough, to use other measures to be paid a bonus is there and continues to be there, and it is key that the culture of the company fights that.

Human nature, you can say more specifically, greed, to beat the competition no matter what is probably at the outset of that.

That does not do away with the fact that corruption is bad. The question for all of us is what can we do about it. I think it is a whole set of different approaches.

First transparency has an impact.

Second, claw-back measures that will take away a bonus if it comes out it was achieved through means other than integrity, may be very effective in preventing wrongdoing.

Third, I believe increased enforcement measures that are taken and that we see based on the increased laws both affecting public and private corruption coming up increasingly on a global level should have the deterring effect on at least some of these people that think rationally and would say the risk of being caught is getting higher. If I am getting caught, the cost is so much higher than what I benefit from it that I probably should not be doing it.

I end by stating that which is also the topic for today: what can we or what can you do in your daily life as arbitrators to help rein in the risk of corruption? With that, I thank you for your attention and turn back to Maxi.

**MAXI SCHERER:**

I know that Mark has a comment. I might have a quick question for you as well in terms of the list that you have given us. One of the previous slides had this list of absolutely tremendous crimes under the FCPA. We are all aware of those, but the public conscience or even non-specific white-collar crime lawyers do not necessarily have a conscious knowledge of the fact that there are actually equally hefty fines filed under other enforcement mechanisms. We heard before about other enforcement mechanisms against corruption, but these top fines that have you under the FCPA enforcement actions – do they have an equivalent under other mechanisms, or is it that we talk more about the FCPA because it is sexier?

**THOMAS WERLEN:**

Clearly, the US had to come to the table to get things happening. If we look at the settlement now that was reached with Odebrecht, which would have been 3.2 billion, but the company was insolvent, so it was reduced to 2 billion, out of that – this is a separate situation – if every country went after corruption against the same company at the same time, you would imagine there is a competition about who gets the money, and the US is often first.

Odebrecht is a good example of some alignment of Swiss, Brazilian and US DOJs to first go after the wrongdoing. In that distribution, a large part of the money, and the DOJ agreed to that, went to Brazil. That is why Odebrecht does not show up on that list, but it shows the DOJ ones.

Clearly based on the fact that the US started with these – and it is something that people do not necessarily like – you know that. When you are a bank in the US or a company in the US selling to the government, you cannot afford an indictment, and so at some point, you need to deal with the settlement, and the richer you are, the more you can pay, and there is a bargain about that. That is why the possibility of indictment and EPAs against a company, not against an individual, is a huge weapon that the US has.

We see that countries for the last ten years, France for instance, have now started following that path. We would know Switzerland is considering it, that the corporate criminal liability out of Roman or German law [Societas delinquere non potest] is maybe going away. Only if you start with that, you would see higher fines. It is against the nature of civil law, but it might overhaul criminal and European law. It may change down the road; otherwise, if you do not have fines, you do not get these people to stop doing it.

**MARK PIETH:**

You rightly mention that there are alternatives, sanctions, mechanisms, which companies are quite afraid of. My experience has been, as Chairman of the Sanctions Board of the African Development Bank, debarment is what you are afraid of because you will be forced off the list of people who are allowed to be on it.

What is very tough is that these multinational development banks have agreed to cross the Bar. If the African Bank says you are no longer going to be one of our valid bidders, it has a worldwide effect. It will have an effect in Asia as well, and that could hurt more than a monetary sanction.

A brief comment on the development here. You have mentioned that actually, in this Brazilian case, three countries have gotten together. That is a very new development that one collectively settles with the company. In this case, most of the money went to Brazil, but the US and Switzerland also participated.

In fact, for the Swiss representatives here, it is interesting that one is working on a new article in the Swiss Code of Criminal Procedure that copies basically the American system word by word on how to settle, to make explicit what we all know happens with DOJ and the SEC.

# 'Red Flags' for Identifying Suspicious Relationships

*Michael W. Faske*

**MAXI SCHERER:**

We will continue with our pursuit of setting the scene for the day on the discussion of corruption and arbitration. We now turn to very practical tips on how to identify suspicious relationships. What are the red flags concretely that one should be aware of internally in companies but also more globally?

We are very lucky to have Michael Faske here. As you see, we almost lost him in a ski accident! He is with Ernst & Young. He is the head of the Forensic and Integrity Services Group here in Switzerland. He has over twenty years of experience working in fraud and investigations, particularly fraud prevention and other compliance matters. He is also a guest lecturer at the Lucerne University and the Competence Centre for Forensic and Economic Crime – which sounds very esoteric to me – and also at the European School of Management and Technology. We are very happy to have you.

**MICHAEL FASKE:**

Thank you for the kind introduction. I am glad I do not have to talk about skiing today! Identifying red flags or suspicious relationships, as a forensic investigator, we typically refer to suspicious third parties in general. If you look at the statistics, for example, of the Department of Justice in the US, there is literally no case that was not triggered either by a third party or a major involvement of a third party. If we look at the big cases over the last few years, the biggest risk that a company can face is to do business with people whom you do not really know and/or you are not really comfortable with what they are about to do.

Before I dive deeper into the red flags as mentioned, let me set the scene a little bit by describing the typical dilemma you may face as a corporate but equally as a forensic investigator and probably also a white-collar crime lawyer. It does not matter whether you are investigating a corruption case or you want to do prevention; it is very unlikely that if you push a button or look into something, you will immediately find the corruption.

What is shown here on the chart behind me is that typically everything happens outside this sphere of the company. You have a third party, the fraudster; you typically have a rogue employee or a group of employees who basically do all the communication, all the transaction outside the sphere of the company. When you are talking about an investigation or doing prevention, you are looking for evidence, you are looking for red flags, but in order to do so, you would need an information universe, but the universe you would actually need is outside your reach because, as I said, it takes place outside the sphere of your company. They are using private devices; they are using private bank accounts, private communication channels and so on.

As a company, you can only rely on what I have put in the inner circle with the factory symbol, which is the information found on the devices t that you, as a company, would own. It is typical information like in your ERP system: so transactional data, communication data, emails, other communications like classic mail, fax, mobile devices and so on.

However, as I said, the typical corruption takes place outside, and you, unfortunately, have to rely on the information that you can legally obtain. That is the dilemma that you are always facing, and that is why you have to look for not alternative information but indicators pointing you in the right direction.

When I was preparing for this presentation, I thought that showing you concrete cases or concrete red flags for identifying a suspicious relationship probably does not make sense because depending on the industry, the sector and the business a company is in, these might differ from another. So instead, I decided to give you two examples of the major mistakes companies make when working with third parties.

The first problem that most of the companies I have seen doing is that they do not know what their third party is like. They do not have an established internal third-party risk management process. A very high-level process these days, as illustrated in the chart behind me, would start with: what is the onboarding process of a third party? Do I have the basic information about this third party, such as what is the shareholder structure like, what was the last financial statement, where is the location of the company, et cetera? Based on this information, as part of the onboarding process, you would need to validate this information by performing a risk assessment on that information or a due diligence process by taking other information in order to validate the information that I have received. This is basically a concept we are seeing in the non-regulated industries coming from the financial services industries.

You all might know that in the financial services industry, for years, under the anti-money laundering provisions, banks have to adhere to 'know-your-customer' principles (KYC). They need to validate the identity of the customer.

We have seen cases here in Switzerland also, under the Alstom case, for example, where the prosecutor said, 'Listen, you cannot apply for the criminal defence because you did not do professional due diligence on your agents.

You did not really know what the conduct of these agents was.' They are applying the concept of KYC from the banking world and the non-regulated industries.

Once you have this industry information on the third party, you want to ensure that you can proceed with contracting. For example, do you have a right to audit? If you have an agent in Malaysia or in Ukraine, do you periodically visit them and have an understanding of what their business conduct is like? As you can see, it is a kind of a wheel starting from contracting to monitoring, mitigating and dealing with the risk until termination, if needed, if there is a real breach of this conduct.

Typical due diligence on customers today is performed professionally. They typically use compliance databases. There are professional and commercial databases like World-Check, World Compliance, et cetera. There are business databases like Creditreform, Thompson Reuters. There are also country-specific databases. In Switzerland, we have Zefix or Moneyhouse. This is all publicly available information that you could get to validate third party information.

The goal is, as shown here, to get the information about third party relating to reputation, credentials, history of operations - have they been engaged in bribery cases, and so on.

The takeaway from this point is that a lot of companies are lacking an understanding of their counterparty with whom they are dealing because they are not asking these questions.

The second more risky part of all this is an internal question. Many companies do not really know what their interaction with a third party really is. Not that I do not know who the party is, but what is my business with that third party?

If you take this picture as an analogy, you see the normal path here, and here another word for the path is a process. This would be, under the company's understanding, my process and the gate would be a control, but you see what happens here in this way in the park. It is not convenient for people to walk through the gates, so they just bypass it.

How it looks then in the company internally is like this - the lasagne versus spaghetti. It is what I have shown here; it is a classic procurement-to-pay process. It starts with issuing a process order, getting the terms and conditions negotiated, signing the contract, getting the contract approved, sending an invoice, getting the goods delivered and so on.

Companies typically, on the left side, believe it is a linear process, and in the critical elements of my process, I have control, like in the picture before, and then it works. The risk is mitigated. The reality is actual; it is the spaghetti process. There is hardly any process that works linearly and where the controls always work.

In order to show you that this is not just made up by me, that this is reality, I want to give you a living example of a customer where we analysed the procurement-to-pay process and basically took for one fiscal year, all financial transactions in this procurement-to-pay process and ran them through data analytics.

What you will see in a second is a movie or a fast motion summary. We took thousands of transactions, dumped them in the tool and analysed the internal flow using modern data analytics. This process is called process mining. To do this, you are not only taking the transaction itself but also taking the metadata, such as who released this transaction; when was it released; when did it go from A to B; what happened after B; did it go to C or D, and so on. Then you can very nicely visualise the transaction flow.

As I said, in fast time, all transactions for this company looked like the spaghetti process.

You see, there are a lot of bubbles running through this process. If I pause here for a second, you can already see the bubbles are bounding around from process step to process step. You also see different colours. At this moment, this is a really comprehensive view. You see the darker blue ones, which are more driven by a single transaction, then you also see transaction areas that were lesser-used and not so important or maybe exceptional transactions and so on.

I can then drill into this process and look at it from a fraud perspective and only look at the riskiest processes. I can sort them linear at the moment, but then I can look at the most important parts of my procurement process, like the approval, and then I drill down and look at the exceptions.

It looks, when I run the movie again, from the high-level transaction flow, I now can look at the most important process and how the transactions flow within these processes. If I then drill in deeper and look at the exceptions within these seven most important controls and processes, very soon, I will see there is, at the top level, one exception running through, which is most likely a timing problem. If you have, in addition to this, real proof, then it becomes a financial irregularity or problem.

At the bottom, you see there is one transaction coming up very soon, from payment going up to signing the contract. You see that one single transaction was moving up. That is a transaction where the payment was released, and we figured out that it did not pass the assignment process. What we then did was to click or look deeper into this process and looked at all the details of that single transaction. We quickly see there is one approver approving payments without a contract and without signature.

What you then can do is to run certain other forensic analytics on this single transaction, and specifically on the approver, and enquire with whom this single-user worked? I have this transaction now. I click deeper in, and I see the user is the FYLC. We analysed it and looked at this specific user who was making the payment: what is his universe? What is the social universe in the company?

You see now all these transactions by users. It turned out that basically, this one user collusively worked together with another user in finance and controlling. Basically, there were two people working collusively to get payments through the system without signatures, without approvals and so on.

The short story of this exhaustive process is coming back to dealing with third parties, understanding what is my third party, what is the conduct, who is the underlying beneficial owner, but then actually what is my business with this third party?

When it comes to red flags, a lot of companies are not doing their homework of really understanding their own business, their own processes and their own third parties. In this case, we identified the risk of segregation of duties, overriding manual processes, duplicate payments, approval after payment runs and passing the payments without the second-level approval.

**MAXI SCHERER:**

We are still digesting all of what Michael has just told us. I saw some faces in the audience - this is absolutely fascinating. I guess that is what you get if you invite a forensic head of analytics: you get very, very worried.

One question that immediately popped up in my head, and I would like to ask not only the panel but also the audience and potentially as a thing for the subsequent panels - how much of that is our duty as arbitrators or as arbitration counsel? Do we have a duty to use these professional compliance databases in which we can find out what these third parties are doing? Have they been involved in bribery? Can we use some of this very professional information out there to know more about our clients, either the clients that we represent in our arbitration or the clients, i.e., the parties, before us if we sit as arbitrators?

I do not want to give you the answer, but here is the question that pops up in my head if any of you would like to comment from the audience also in terms of the arbitrators.

**MARK PIETH:**

I am tempted to try to sharpen it a bit. Imagine you have an agent's contract. Very typical it would say three things: 'I am going to provide market information', fair enough. 'I am also going to engage in marketing, and I am also going to provide legal support.' Then immediately, the question would be, 'Hang on, can this small outfit with one person actually do all that in a difficult market?' Then the immediate next question is, 'What would I want to do if I wanted to know more in the arbitration situation? Can I actually motivate the tribunal to go back to the other party and say, "Could you show the work product?" If they are reluctant to cooperate, can you then say negative inferences? Does that work for you?'

**MAXI SCHERER:**

I promised you some time for questions and comments from the audience, and I think it is now time. I would like to make a little twist to our rules. Obviously, we have a transcript, and I would ask you to say your name and affiliation when you ask questions, but I would also like you to be allowed to ask questions that you can take off the transcript. This is a sensitive topic. If you want to make any questions or comments that we can then take off the transcript, I would like to invite you to also make those comments or ask those questions. With that in mind, I am sure there are microphones somewhere in the audience.

This is usually quite a lively audience, and this is why I was so mindful of the fact that I would like to make you comfortable in asking them. Obviously, you can broaden the topic - I know this is an audience of arbitration lawyers - to more corruption arbitration-related questions. Please feel free.

**THIERRY LINARES:**

Just to remark from the presentation of Mr Werlen, that most transactions about corruption are outside the control sphere of the company, whereas the investigations, as presented by Mr Faske, are, of course, from internal data, I guess. How do those two facets work in investigations? How do you really investigate when it is outside the sphere of the company? Data analytics do not work that well.

**THOMAS WERLEN:**

If you are actually a company as such, if you do an internal investigation, as you say, you are bound to look at the materials that are within the company. We do not have Mr Bertossa here today, but unlike the Public Prosecutor, they can also access third parties, whatever they need.

If your question is what are the limitations of internal investigations, there you are. Obviously, having said that, if you have millions of emails and you have forensic support that allows you to cut to the chase quite quickly, also you see where you have leads against third parties, often in these investigations, the company is cooperating with prosecutors and in that sense would obviously share the information out of the joint investigation with prosecutors; that they do what they need to do in order to get that information that is beyond the company's scope.

I do not want to do a white-collar seminar today, but it is an excellent question as to how internal and public investigations work together and their ups and downs. I do not want to go into that topic.

**MICHAEL FASKE:**

Many times when you conduct an internal investigation, you are coming to a point where you feel the information is not exhaustive. It might be a strategic decision from the company to file a criminal complaint and seek the support of prosecutors and law enforcement. From the private investigation perspective, from a company's perspective, that is a big dilemma you are facing.

**THOMAS WERLEN:**

You certainly have contracts with third parties that allow you to ask for some information, but if the other side does not cooperate, you cannot force them. You are not stuck at the company's borders legally; you can go out and would do, but they might not cooperate, and that is where you need the public prosecutor.

**ANDREA MEIER:**

I was interested in learning about your experience if it comes to preventive measures of companies and how you assess the current status. We talked about preventive measures in fighting corruption. In your perception, Thomas Werlen and Michael

Faske, do you think the companies do enough nowadays in monitoring their compliance and fighting corruption? Is there still a tendency sometimes to turn a blind eye in the hope of short-term gains from possible corrupt behaviour?

**THOMAS WERLEN:**

I do not know whether that is a question for the transcript or not. It depends; let us start with regulated industries. You mentioned the financial industry. They should have done third party checks, as we know, and notwithstanding that we now have some huge money laundering issues that actually happened from 2015 to 2018 in connection with Venezuela, for instance. That is one question, even if you are forced by regulators to do so.

Second, even in a non-regulated industry, as you called it Michael, you have, and I think many large and global companies are clearly aware of that. The question – are you a global company subject to US enforcement? – that is one question very often looked into.

Going one step down, I think really the way to prevent it is a question of the culture that you see coming out. It should not be that you just act because the law environment tells you to do it, that is section one, or you might be called an outlaw. You need to bring about a culture.

Here we clearly see improvement; I would say – I obviously open up to my colleagues on the panel – over the last ten or fifteen years for various reasons. There are clearly also some industries in particular where I would say there are a lot of issues from the past, and actually, a lot of companies that want to make a change are also in a bind because they have a lot of baggage from the past. If you start to do it, you can also bring down the company if you do it wrong, so that is an issue that I see as well.

**MICHAEL FASKE:**

What you are not supposed to forget is corruption is a deliberate act. People are doing it willingly, meaning willingly circumventing the controls. When we are talking about preventing bribery and corruption, it has two elements: on the one side is the controls element, and we have seen it in the M&A sphere that many companies are lacking really understanding their internal processes and controls properly; but the second element is the internal culture rather than only processes and controls. How do I shape the culture in order to create an environment so that people are doing the right thing?

What we have seen, specifically after the Siemens scandal, is an increase in classic compliance activity. In the beginning, it was really this classic rules-based compliance mostly. Forgive me the sentence, but legal folks were sitting there transcribing laws into internal policy and thinking now that we are creating a culture. This exercise pretty much failed over the last ten years. What we see now is a shift from classic rules-based compliance into more principle-based ethics and integrity.

There is a lot of debate not only in academia but also in companies, and a lot of companies struggle about how to implement it. What does it mean to act in an ethical and integral way? The difficulty as a corporate is always how do I measure it? How do I implement it? You need to bake it in your people process. You have to incentivise people, but how do you measure people with an ethical background? That is the big question mark for everybody at the moment: how to shape a culture to act purely ethical and to do the right thing?

**MARK PIETH:**

Thomas, in his presentation, mentioned the incentive structure for employees. That is a fundamental point.

Maybe by way of experience, I was asked to be a compliance monitor over a German construction company with 130,000 people for the US Army. Everything looked very good. They had a fantastic compliance system, and it looked as if they were following the compliance system. They did all the training and everything. The problem was there was no solution for the bonus or lack of bonus if you did not make the deal. You had a target, and if you did not make the target, you had less salary. That kind of issue was not picked up. The problem is then you kind of miss not addressing the difficulty of the employee finding himself in this sandwich position.

**MAXI SCHERER:**

A long time ago, I was part of a large team of lawyers doing some FCPA training in a company that has been fined by the US. We trained in different jurisdictions the people actually selling the products of that company. That is exactly what we heard each time that we went out to meet. The people said, 'Your rules are nice and good, but I need to make my target, and in order to get my target if everyone else sticks to a certain standard in this country, it would be very difficult for me to do otherwise.' This is something that people said in between sessions, never in sessions. Definitely changing the remuneration structure and the economic incentives for those doing the deals is certainly an important aspect.

I find this entire topic absolutely fascinating. I hope we set the scene on some of the aspects and some of the concepts and questions that we are now going to continue to discuss over the day, more in relation to arbitration, but I would particularly like to thank the panel.

# Panel 2: Impact of Corruption on Substantive Matters

*Moderated by Mariella Orelli*

**CHRISTIAN OETIKER:**

We now come to panel 2, which deals with the impact of corruption on substantive matters. Panel 2 will be led by Mariella Orelli. She is a partner in Homburger's Litigation and Arbitration team in Zurich. She holds degrees from the University of Zurich and the College of Europe in Bruges.

*Chambers Global* said she is wonderful, and we will have the opportunity to test that today. *Chambers*, in particular, also highlighted that Mariella goes into detail and gets to the point, so we will also check that out today.

In her CV, you will note that in addition to the arbitration, litigation, competition and insurance team, Mariella is also in Homburger's Brazilian team. I am sure she is wearing the shirt with the number 10, so the floor is yours.

**MARIELLA ORELLI:**

Thank you for reminding me of the flattering quote. If it is written there, I would say it must be true. If the implication is that I bribed somebody for making that statement, that implication is rejected forcefully!

Thank you to the audience for coming back right on time for this session to take place without major delay. The topic of the session is the impact of corruption on substantive issues.

We will look not only at issues associated with allegations of corruption that arise in the preliminary stage of arbitration but also obviously at issues associated with allegations of corruption that arise at the merit stage of arbitration. We will do so in relation to both commercial arbitration as well with regard to investment arbitration.

This is possible because we have the honour of having among our speakers today Andrea Menaker. I would like to introduce her to you. She is a partner at White & Case. She was based in Washington DC but she is currently moving to London. She is one of the few lawyers here in Europe that can boast a twenty-year-long experience working exclusively in investment arbitration matters. According to the website, she represents equally respondent states and the claimant investors. I tried to understand what the secret is for keeping that balance, but I have not got a satisfactory answer. We may hear more about that later on. Prior to joining private practice, Andrea was lead counsel for the US in Chapter 11 arbitrations. She will certainly be best placed to deal with the impact of corruption in investment arbitration.

The second speaker I would like to introduce to you is Professor Christoph Müller. Professor Christoph Müller is a Professor at the Faculty of Law of the University of Neuchâtel. He teaches contract law, including comparative private law, and is best placed to look at the impact of corruption on the validity of the contract, including the applicable law to those issues.

Most of us are not young enough to know Christoph from his lectures at university, but we know him from his extensive practice as an arbitrator. He has been involved in more than a hundred arbitrations, and I have had the pleasure of sitting together with him on a panel, so we are very happy to have him on this panel.

Last but not least, I would like to introduce the third speaker of our panel, Dr Nikolaus Pitkowitz of Graf & Pitkowitz, a leading firm in Vienna which he has co-founded and which can boast a flourishing practice in arbitration bringing international work to Vienna. He regularly acts as counsel but also as arbitrator, as a chair or as a party-appointed arbitrator, and is well known in Switzerland because he is a very fierce sponsor of Vienna arbitration and the Vienna Rules, but today we have agreed that he will deal with the topic we have asked him to deal with in a neutral manner. He will enlighten us about the issues associated with corruption allegations in arbitration that arise at the early stage of arbitration.

# The Tribunal's Jurisdiction and the Arbitrability of Issues of Corruption

*Niklaus Pitkowitz*

**NIKOLAUS PITKOWITZ:**

Thank you for this kind introduction. I must say as an Austrian, as a Viennese, I am particularly honoured I have been invited here to speak on corruption, even more in front of this esteemed audience.

Ten years ago, I was first asked to chair a panel on corruption at a conference in Ukraine, in Kyiv, and when we discussed this, suddenly a lady stood up and said, 'This is so fascinating. The first time here corruption is publicly discussed. I am the head of the Ukrainian Anti-corruption Agency, and I find this great.'

This made me quite nervous, and I changed my flight back to Vienna to an earlier flight.

My second event on corruption was a few years later in Azerbaijan. We were also discussing corruption issues, and I was alluding to the Transparency Index of corruption in the judicial system, which has a scale from 0 to 5.

Zero is not corrupt at all, and five is absolutely corrupt. I was making some remarks and saying 'This country has 4.5', and then another lady stood up, and she looked really insulted, and she said, 'This is absolutely wrong. We do not have 4.5; we have 5.0. We are absolutely corrupt.'

Equipped with this experience, I thank the organisers for their confidence that an Austrian would be suitable to address this topic here and properly react to audience intervention.

Clearly, corruption is around, and it has found its way into arbitration, but how to deal with it. Do arbitral tribunals have jurisdiction to hear corruption cases? Here this can be answered with a clear yes. Arbitral tribunals, in general, do have jurisdiction.

There is one old case quoted of 1963 ICC 1110 by the Swedish Judge Lagergren, who had a different view on that, but this is no longer maintained. I think it can be clearly said that the prevailing doctrine, and rightfully, says under the doctrine of separability that arbitration agreements are usually included as arbitration clauses into the main contract, and the arbitration agreement is legally distinct and, therefore, does not necessarily share the same legal state as the main contract. Thus, even if the main contract is tainted by corruption and invalid, the arbitration agreement is not automatically invalid. Consequently, the arbitral tribunals do not lose their jurisdiction powers simply because one party alleges that the contract is void or voidable.

There is one important exception. One can say that there is no automatic presumption of jurisdiction. There are certain circumstances that may invalidate the main contract, and that also affects the arbitration agreement. In fact, there could be cases of direct impeachment of the arbitration agreement if that is individually attacked if the arbitration agreement is directly attacked. An argument is made that according to the doctrine of competence-competence also, an arbitral tribunal has the power and the ability to assess whether the invalidity of the underlying contract also affects the validity of the arbitration agreement.

An arbitration agreement might be invalid in cases of threat of juris, of forgery or where a party's true consent is lacking. However, I think those are the minority of cases and engaging in corruption, and bribery usually does not affect the party's consent to arbitrate. I think it is rather on the contrary that corrupt parties rather wish to have arbitration clauses to avoid courts.

Whether or not arbitration has jurisdiction also depends on the scope of the arbitration agreement, on the wording of the arbitration clause. I think here the international prevailing view is that reasonable parties intended to give their arbitration clauses a broad scope. There is a pro-arbitration presumption which means that corruption claims will typically and usually be covered by the arbitration.

The good news is that, in general, arbitral tribunals have jurisdiction to hear corruption cases in commercial cases. The bad news is we will have to deal with those. That could be one way to address that if, prior to the limit, the arbitrator also wants to test the arbitrability of corruption-tainted disputes.

Generally, arbitrability is defined by whether a certain dispute is capable of settlement by arbitration. National states retain certain subject matters for the courts. Typically also, the law applicable to this question of arbitrability is the *lex arbitri*, the law in front of the seat where the question arises.

There could be, of course, as we all know, certain categories of disputes which are not arbitrable, tax, trade, competition, consumer claims, employment, but disputes involving claims of corruption, bribery or similar illegality I think it is now generally seen and considered, and rightly so, that those must be seen as arbitrable. They are only very limited, and I only found one case law where the Pakistani court held otherwise.

What does that mean? It means that the jurisdiction, the arbitrability, gives the arbitral tribunal the power to impose criminal sanctions. It is as Alexis Mourre put it, in arbitration, criminal provisions are no more and no less than mandatory rules. That means the criminal parties reserve for the criminal authorities and, just as civil courts, arbitral tribunals have the power to draw the civil consequences of illicit behaviour in a business dispute.

That principle has constantly been upheld, and as recently as in 2015, an English Court of Appeal decision in the *London Steamship Mutual Insurance Association v. Kingdom of Spain.* It is clear that the arbitrator has the power to draw civil consequences of the rule of the criminal law on the business dispute, and it is the arbitrator's duty to determine illegality, fraud and collusion and draw the consequences therefrom.

Another aspect that often arises is parallel criminal and parallel arbitration proceedings and how to deal with them. Is there *lis pendens,* is there a limit? Again, here, the general view, which I find correct, is that criminal proceedings must not be considered to limit an ongoing arbitration in any way, even if this arbitration is dealing with the same set of facts.

Again, as to any general rule, there is an exception. One exception could be the case where the same request for relief that is sought in the criminal proceedings is also sought in the arbitration proceedings. There was a case, *Thomson-CSF v. Republic of China Navy,* in which a French court had to deal with that. It found that there was no waiver of the right to pursue reparation under the arbitration because, in the French criminal proceedings, there was no request made for a monetary award, and hence the claim was then ultimately rejected in the criminal proceedings.

That could be difficult in jurisdictions like Austria and Switzerland where one has an opportunity to also file monetary claims in front of criminal authorities; so in such a case, that could potentially give rise to an implied waiver of the arbitration agreement if those parallel proceedings are being pursued.

Another question if there are parallel proceedings is that can those be stayed because very often, and evidently, an arbitral tribunal is not equipped with means like criminal courts. It cannot sentence persons to appear. You do not have any search warrant issues, so one can say that often happens in that situation – why do you not interrupt the arbitration pending the outcome of the criminal proceedings?

Again, here I think the general view is that criminal law should not be allowed to disrupt a lawful arbitration. The tribunal does not have a duty – it has a right perhaps, but it does not have a duty – to stay proceedings if parallel criminal proceedings are pending before a court, and that flows from two general principles: one is the obligation of arbitrators to conduct the proceedings in an expeditious way, which is an inherent obligation when accepting to act as an arbitrator; and, second, the parties' election to settle a dispute in front of an arbitral tribunal.

Even in France, which had this long-standing principle that criminal actions hold civil actions in check, I understand there is a rethinking now, and it is clear that arbitral proceedings have the right to prevail. That has also been confirmed by a 2007 decision of the Federal Tribunal of Switzerland that there is a discretion to stay but no obligation.

Theobald Naud has determined eight, which I find very valuable, criteria which need to be looked at when you find out as an arbitral tribunal whether you should exercise that discretion. Do the allegations go to the core of the dispute? What is the status of the criminal proceedings and stake in the overall criminal proceedings? Is the tribunal able to determine the likely timing of decisions in criminal matters? It could be going on for years. Can the criminal decision be challenged on appeal? The timing of the petition to stay the proceedings was it made to delay the proceedings? The timing that perceived independence of the authorities dealing with criminal proceedings. Is the criminal process likely to produce further relevant evidence? Can either party use the filing of criminal complaints as a tactical weapon? I think that is very comprehensive.

With that general framework, I would now conclude with some strategic considerations. How to attack a corrupt-tainted contract? Here even though, as I just said, there is a power, an obligation, an opportunity, it appears, based on the study which was made by Cecily Rose in 2014, that the majority of arbitral tribunals try to evade having to deal with corruption. That is, of course, a surprise. Cecily Rose reviewed more than fifty awards and found that '*the role that arbitral tribunals are playing in determining whether corruption has occurred remains minimal and unsatisfactory*'. They seem to avoid the difficult task of ruling on corruption in a lot of cases by jurisdictional manoeuvres. What is the lesson to be drawn from that, from a strategic point of view? It is wise, I think, to also consider on each side either giving the tribunal an escape route on the jurisdictional side or trying to block that if you want to force it to deal with that.

Corruption-tainted contracts are usually null and void, and I will not go into that detail here.

I just want to conclude with a case I was recently involved in, which is a matter in which our client, a Baltic financial institution, was claiming a repayment of funds it had lost as a result of corruption. Very simplified, a shareholder of our client had prompted our client to enter into a sham transaction containing an arbitration clause under which it made a substantial payment to an intermediary and then from that intermediary to the thief.

As a result, the financial institution went into bankruptcy because there was a very significant amount of money that was passed on to the thief. The Insolvency Administrator filed a claim against the intermediary, which was another financial institution seated in Vienna, for repayment of those funds and that claim was filed in the Baltic.

What the intermediary did, and that was a very smart move, they filed a torpedo arbitration in Vienna based on their arbitration agreement. That was very smart for two reasons: First of all, under Austrian law, which implemented the UNCITRAL model law, the arbitration has absolute priority over litigation, so the Austrian arbitral tribunal had little means to deny jurisdiction; and, second, the Austrian arbitral tribunal did not have the means to find out if there is corruption or not because the intermediary, as the claimant, were the ones who were setting the evidence to be presented.

The firm represented the Baltic insolvency institution, and we had a dual strategy on what you have heard now. We said we try to give the arbitral tribunal an escape route, say it does not hold jurisdiction, the Baltic claims do not really fall under the arbitration agreement; and, second, we tried to set up a list of red flags because we did not have any evidence at hand - a list of red flags indicating that there was in fact corruption. I am very pleased to say that the award was released last week. We were fortunate that we had a very experienced and also robust Swiss chair who took this obligation to deal with corruption really serious. The tribunal denied jurisdiction, and it found the transaction was void for corruption.

With that, I hope I am still welcome here. I confidently booked the late flight home to Vienna! Thank you very much.

**MARIELLA ORELLI:**

Thank you for your view on the issues connected with the allegations of corruption arising at the preliminary stage and also for sharing, in a lively manner, your experience with those cases.

I would like to follow up on one of the strategic considerations that you mentioned. I think you essentially were saying that parties who want to invoke bribery or illegality to void the contract, to get the contract nullified, are well-advised to also plead nullity based on other legal grounds because tribunals are rather reluctant to accept allegations of corruption. I think this is a fair statement, and the statistics you have mentioned fully confirm that it is fair to say arbitral tribunals tend to accept allegations of corruption only in cases in which corruption is manifest, in cases in which the evidence is overwhelming.

I would like to hear from you, but certainly also from other colleagues who are acting very often as arbitrators, as to whether the reluctance of the arbitral tribunals when it comes to tackling corruption is justified or whether we should actually expect arbitral tribunals to take a different approach and to approach allegations of corruption with more courage.

**NIKOLAUS PITKOWITZ:**

Alluding to this case, I must say this was a parallel case, and there had been a previous case when another arbitral tribunal had done exactly the opposite and had found that it holds jurisdiction, but there is no corruption with absolutely the same circumstances around. I think there is still this tendency of trying to evade dealing with corruption.

We have seen, particularly in Austria – that is one of the reasons I was invited – quite a lot of contracts, particularly with participants in countries from the former Soviet Union where corruption is brought up as an issue. My experience is when that is brought up as the main issue, typically, the arbitral tribunals deal with that with few exceptions.

**MARIELLA ORELLI:**

From the floor, are there any contributions on this topic? Can we expect or should we expect arbitral tribunals to take a stronger stance when it comes to corruption?

**ANNE VERONIQUE SCHLAEPFER:**

I think the situation has changed a lot in the course of the last ten to twenty years. Nowadays, I think tribunals are much more concerned by issues of corruption, and you see awards in which the issue is really addressed very clearly. We all know even the standard of proof has changed, and very often now arbitral tribunals do not consider anymore that you have to have a high threshold to prove corruption because if you have a high threshold, you will never be able to prove corruption as it is, by definition, hidden or concealed otherwise there is no real corruption. This has changed.

I think this view which maybe some tribunals still have, is not the majority view nowadays. Now the idea is rather - and maybe we go too far in the other direction - to take this issue very seriously, and if there are suspicions that corruption exists, tribunals will deal with it and very often will take strong decisions. This has changed a lot. The mentality has changed a lot in the course of the last few years.

**CHRISTOPH MÜLLER:**

I think in parallel, the mentality has changed but also the fact that criminal means have not been successful during the last twenty years, over the last century. We are more and more aware that perhaps civil means might be more powerful in fighting corruption, and when it comes to civil means, arbitral tribunals cannot any longer say that is none of my business. That is our business, civil means, to fight corruption. It is also this awareness.

**MARIELLA ORELLI:**

Andrea, would you like to enlighten us on your observations regarding the stance of arbitral tribunals in investment arbitration cases?

**ANDREA MENAKER:**

I think that in investment arbitration cases, as Anne Veronique has said, when the issue is front and centre before the tribunal, they deal with it. They have to. It is usually a big issue that is in front of them.

I also think there is a recognition that because corruption is hidden and concealed that tribunals today rather almost uniformly have accepted that it may be proven by circumstantial evidence and that they do look at these red flags we have heard about.

All of that said, while not imposing a higher standard of proof than is imposed to prove other facts of the case, as had sometimes been suggested, the tribunal still has to find that it is more probable than not that corruption has occurred, and that is still difficult to prove.

That is still what they are ultimately faced with.

Yes, in some circumstances, if there is another jurisdictional issue, they may choose to deal with that one but, if not - and this is a big jurisdictional issue and the rest are merits defences - you will see them dealing with it head-on and whether or not they find it will ultimately depend on evidence that is put forward.

**MARIELLA ORELLI:**

The comments we have received so far are largely positive as to the status of arbitration or the attitude of arbitral tribunals in cases in which allegations of corruption are raised. Is there anybody in the audience who believes that tribunals should do even more than what they are doing currently, or are we all positive that the actual current status is good enough?

**KATE DAVIES:**

I am sorry to burst the bubble, but my own experience of corruption issues arising in an arbitral context is that tribunals are not sufficiently willing to investigate them. They are forced to investigate them, particularly in an investment context where corruption defences on the part of states, particularly in certain parts of the world, do frequently come up. They do frequently come up in those parts of the world because corruption is endemic. In certain parts of the world, in sub-Asian continental countries, 95 % of the people in some of those jurisdictions will admit to either having offered or taken a bribe. These problems are endemic, so it is not a surprise that corruption comes up as a defence endemically in investor-state arbitrations dealing with those states.

My experience is, yes, they are dealing with them because they have been forced to deal with them, but there is still – and maybe this is partly generational, and to echo the professor who spoke first this morning – there is a reluctance on the part of arbitrators, in my experience, to really engage with what it is that corruption is, how difficult it is to prove, and what the international communities' approach to corruption is.

There is an arbitral-centric approach to corruption, in my experience, and there is a lack of willingness to engage with what the criminal community is doing in relation to corruption and what evidence it is that the criminal community would accept as evidencing corruption.

For example, in the criminal context, if you have payments to an agent in relation to a particular contract for which there are no receipts and no invoices, that is automatically a presumption – that is a corrupt payment. I have experience of that issue arising in an arbitral context where in excess of USD 1 million worth of payments to an agent were completely unevidenced, and that was not accepted as being prima facie evidence of a bribe.

There is a disconnect. I am pleased to see this conference today bringing together the white-collar world and the arbitral world because I think that is what needs to happen. I think the arbitral world needs to be educated by the white-collar world as to what corruption is and how it is to be dealt with.

**SPEAKER FROM THE FLOOR:**

[Name requested to be withheld]. Arbitration, in general, is under attack with criticism against investment arbitration; now, it transpires also in commercial arbitration. I think that if we want to preserve arbitration as a means to resolve disputes, we have to face our responsibilities, and we have to address those issues of corruption if they arise. It would be extremely bad for our job not to do it because we have to give clear answers to the criticism of corruption. This is one area where this criticism would be justified if arbitrators would simply put allegations under the carpet and not deal with them.

**MARIELLA ORELLI:**

Thank you for your contributions. Obviously, there are different ways to look at the stance of arbitral tribunals when it comes to allegations of corruption. What I am sure we all agree on is that events such as this conference help us, when acting as arbitrators, as well as when acting as counsel, to be more aware and sensitised about the importance of these kinds of issues.

With that, I turn to Professor Christoph Müller, who will talk about the impact of corruption on the validity of the contract.

# The Impact of Corruption on the Contract, Including the Issue of Applicable Law

*Christoph Müller*

**CHRISTOPH MÜLLER:**

Ladies and gentlemen, good morning. We heard this morning from Professor Pieth that professors do not prepare PowerPoint presentations. I am the only one in the second panel to have one, so we are now equal!

I will shortly introduce the following two subjects: first, which law governs the existence and the consequences of corruption; and, second, what impact does corruption have on the contract. The first question concerning the applicable law only arises where there are differences between the potentially applicable laws. This will not likely be the case when there is outright bribery of government officials. No so-called 'civilized' country will tolerate such a clear case of corruption. However, a true conflict can arise in disputes involving intermediary agreements which contemplate the exercise of influence over government officials. In such a context, corruption typically involves the following four parties: first, the person or entity which seeks to obtain the main contract and who provides the bribe (I call this person or entity 'the (corrupting) principal'); second, the person or entity which acts on behalf of this principal (I call this person or entity 'the (corrupting) intermediary'); third, the person who is able to influence the award of the main contract and who receives the bribe (I call this person 'the (corrupted) official'); and last but not least the entity which enters into the main contract with the principal (I call this entity simply 'the government').

These four actors are linked by various contractual relationships. For the time being, I will focus on the first one; I call it the intermediary agreement between the principal and the intermediary. This agreement is a contract pursuant to which the intermediary is engaged by the principal to assist in procuring the government contract for the latter.

The law applicable to such agreements is also almost never the same law as the law of the country in which the main contract will be awarded. They also typically provide for the seat of the arbitration to be outside of this country. If the law chosen by the parties to govern their agreement does not have the same approach to the intermediary agreements and to corruption in general as the law of the country awarding the main contract, or the law of the seat of the arbitration, there might be a genuine conflict of laws issue.

Let us take a concrete example that is inspired by the famous *Hilmarton* case. In this case, there was an intermediary agreement between a French corporation and an English intermediary to be performed in Algeria. The English intermediary negotiates with the Algerian government officials in order to procure for the French principal a construction contract in Algeria.

The intermediary agreement is governed by Austrian law and provides for arbitration in Switzerland. Anti-corruption regulations under Algerian law at the time of the *Hilmarton* case - and I am not sure if it is still the case today - prohibited the recourse to intermediaries in government procurement, whereas, as you know, Austrian and Swiss law do not, at least not per se. For the sake of convenience, let us assume that the arbitral tribunal sitting in Switzerland applies Swiss conflict of laws rules. I know that this is open to discussion as well but for this case, let us simplify matters. These Swiss conflict of laws rules will determine whether the circumstances call for the parties' chosen law (i.e., Austrian law) to be overridden by the public policy rules of the place of performance (i.e., Algerian law) or that of the seat (i.e., Swiss law).

The first candidate is the place of performance, i.e., Algerian law. Frequently, and in case it is the same, the intermediary agreement will have little or no connection with the jurisdiction of the chosen law, which in this case is Austria. In *Hilmarton*, the French principal and the English intermediary had no connection whatsoever with Austria. They are instead more closely related to the place of performance, i.e., Algeria.

Some jurisdictions provide that public policy consideration expressed through mandatory laws, or *lois de police* at the place of performance can override the law chosen by the parties if they have a sufficiently close connection to the parties' dispute. Arbitral tribunals, for instance, sitting in Switzerland, must apply foreign mandatory rules under Article 187 PILA. However, even under Swiss law, it remains controversial what preconditions must be satisfied before such rules may be allowed to override the parties' chosen law.

Arbitral tribunals seated in Switzerland have held, a few decades ago now, that foreign mandatory rules which prohibit the use of intermediaries per se do not fulfil the necessary preconditions. In contrast, English law disregards the mandatory laws of the place of performance in favour of the parties' chosen law subject to a number of very limited exceptions.

The second candidate is the law of the arbitral seat, i.e., Swiss law in my example.

Usually, the provisions of the parties' chosen law are not overridden by public policy rules of the law of the forum. The forum as well usually has little or no connection with the contract governed by the foreign law (i.e., Austrian law) and to be performed in a foreign jurisdiction (i.e., Algeria). The exception is where local rules on illegality constitute mandatory forum rules that apply to the contract regardless of the law chosen by the parties. The forum's public policy rules, as opposed to mandatory rules, typically do not override the law chosen by the parties unless again the dispute has a sufficiently close connection with the forum or the public policy contravened is of a fundamental moral nature (whatever this means). These principles are also reflected in the Rome 1 regulation and various provisions.

The last candidate would be transnational public policy. Professor Pieth mentioned it this morning. However, in this context, given the significant differences between jurisdictions regarding the propriety of intermediary agreements, laws prohibiting such agreements do not again reflect 'general principles of morality accepted by all civilised nations'.

In conclusion, it is normally the law chosen by the parties which will govern the question of the existence and the consequences of corruption.

Let me briefly turn to the second topic: the impact of corruption on the contract. The four actors that I have mentioned are typically linked by four legal relationships. The first one is the intermediary agreement that I mentioned before. The intermediary acts on behalf of the principal. The relationship between these two actors is typically an agency or an employment contract.

Second, you have the contract between the intermediary and the official. The intermediary promises certain advantages to the official and, in return, the official promises to ensure that the principal will be awarded the main contract. Let us call this second relationship 'the contract providing for corruption'.

Third, you have a contract between the government and the principal. We can call this contract 'the main contract' or also the 'contract procured by corruption', to be distinguished from the contract providing for corruption.

The main contract is the contract by which the principal obtains the benefit for which the bribe was granted in the first place. Its legal nature may vary and depends on the circumstances.

The last relationship is the one between the government and its corrupted official.

Let us first focus on the contract providing for corruption between the intermediary and the official: 'promesse de pot-de-vin' in French; 'Schmiergeldabsprache' in German. Under most national laws, this contract is null and void as a consequence of its illegal and/or immoral contact. This is in line with Article 8(1) of the Civil Law Convention on Corruption. Article 20(1) of the Swiss Code of Obligations provides the same. You will find similar provisions in the BGB and the French Civil Code. The contract providing for corruption has illegal content because it violates mandatory provisions, including criminal law provisions in the various jurisdictions.

Such a contract has never come, and will never come, into any legal existence. Any party whose situation is influenced by such a contract may invoke the absolute invalidity of these contracts. Interestingly, we had this discussion already, and this will also be a topic this afternoon. Here we have a substantive law provision that tells the arbitrators that they must declare the invalidity of the contract ex officio. Article 20 of the Swiss Code of Obligations provides the same. It is not a procedural duty but a substantive law duty.

What are the consequences of such absolute invalidity? We have to distinguish two situations: first, if the intermediary has not yet paid the bribe, the official cannot claim the payment of the bribe because the contract is null and void.

Second, if the intermediary has already paid the bribe, it should, in principle, be able to claim the restitution of this bribe, be it by a claim for restitution or action for unjust enrichment.

However, under Swiss law and many other laws, this claim for restitution is expressly forbidden. According to Article 66 of the Swiss Code of Obligations: '[n]o right to restitution exists in respect of anything given with a view of producing an unlawful or immoral outcome'. The Swiss Germans have a very poetic word and tongue twister 'Kondiktionssperre' for this principle.

Based on Article 66 of the Swiss Code of Obligations, the intermediary is deprived of its procedural right of action to reclaim the bribe already paid. However, the intermediary's substantive right to the restitution of the bribe survives as an 'obligation naturelle' or 'Naturalobligation'.

This principle is based on various (equitable) maxims, which can be traced back to Roman law. In Common law, the equivalent is the 'clean hands' doctrine.

This solution might, however, lead to an unsatisfactory result. The enriched official may keep the bribe, 'Gauenerlohn' in German and the official cannot be forced to perform the service that it promised in exchange. Therefore, this solution hits only one of the parties to the contract providing for corruption while both the intermediary and the official often seem unworthy of protection.

This is why in other legal systems, such as in England and Wales, illegality rendering a contract void and unenforceable does not automatically bar a claim for the recovery of the benefits conferred under the contract. The court must, in each case, determine whether permitting a claim for restitution of such benefits would be harmful to the integrity of the legal system as a whole.

If the official can keep the bribe, the question arises whether the official must disgorge the bribe to the government. Indeed, crime must not pay: 'bien mal acquis ne profite jamais' or 'das Unrecht soll sich nicht lohnne'.

If the official, as the wrongdoer, is allowed to retain the bribe, even after the offence has been discovered, there will be no effective deterrent. This is why most legal systems entitle the government to bring a claim against the official for the disgorgement of the bribe or a claim for damages.

Some legal systems also allow the government to claim disgorgement of the illegal profits from the principal because by initiating the whole corruption scheme, the principal violates the protected legal sphere of the government – this is the theory at least – which may justify the disgorgement of any legal profits.

Let us finish this short 'tour d'horizon' with the contract procured by corruption, which I also called 'the main contract'. Contrary to the contract providing for corruption, the contract procured by corruption is not necessarily null and void. In most national legal systems, such a contract is merely voidable at the request of the innocent party.

The same holds true from a Swiss law perspective; as such, a contract does not have illegal content. Dubious machinations in the run-up to the contract, which are not reflected in the main contract's content, do not render it illegal or immoral.

However, the government, in particular, can assert that it would not have concluded the main contract if it had known about the corruption. The government can thus call into question the validity of the main contract by invoking the rules on defects of consent ('vices du consentement' or 'Willensmängel'), in particular fraud, and possibly also fundamental error.

Consequently, the government would not be bound, at least under Swiss law, by the main contract (which is affected by a defect in consent) provided that it invalidates the contract within one year of the day on which it discovered the fraud or error.

This is the position under Swiss law.

Article 8(2) of the Civil Law Convention on Corruption contains a similar provision. However, it does not contain a time limit for the assertion of the lack of consent.

What loss could the government claim?

If the government decides not to validate the main contract, and if the parties have not yet performed their obligations, each of the parties would simply be released. This does not prevent the government from claiming damages based on a pre-contractual liability. However, if the government decides not to validate the main contract but the main contract has already been performed in whole or in part, the practical implementation of these principles would be difficult.

In this case, the legal consequences of illegality usually only apply to the future and not to the past. The judge would adapt the content of the main contract so that it reasonably corresponds to what the parties would have agreed to if no bribes had been paid. Typically, this leads to a reduction of the agreed contract price, but it may also lead to further adjustments concerning the obligations of each party.

The loss suffered in this situation consists of the costs that will be incurred in concluding another main contract.

However, the government can also choose to validate the main contract. This would not prevent the government from claiming damages. The loss would consist of the difference between the price of the actual main contract and the bargain that the government could have obtained from the principal in the absence of corruption.

I hope this is enough substantive law food for thought or enough food for substantive law thoughts for a fruitful discussion.

Thank you for your attention.

**MARIELLA ORELLI:**

Thank you, Christoph.

This was an excellent analysis of the contractual relationships among the parties to a corrupt scheme. I do have a follow-up question. My question goes to the state of mind of the principal and whether the state of mind of the principal changes anything to the analysis that you have presented. I am going to tell you where my question comes from.

If you look at corruption schemes, the most basic corruption scheme I think is the one under which the principal itself takes care of the bribe with no involvement of an intermediary. But nowadays, the more developed schemes typically include intermediaries, not just one but many, and certainly many other sophisticated features. I wonder whether the state of mind of the principal plays a role in that analysis and, in particular, whether the principal can defend against a claim of illegality based on corruption by alleging that he was not aware of what the intermediary was doing and he could not expect what the intermediary was doing.

**CHRISTOPH MÜLLER:**

I think for the means of fraud there, you would have to look into the principal's state of mind, whether there was any intent or any negligence to let this fraudulent situation arise.

When it comes to error, I think you would more focus on the government's representative state of mind, and the behaviour or the intent of the principal would not play any role. There could be an error in the government's will to enter into a contract, its consent to the contract, even though there is no fraudulent intent on the principal's side.

**MARIELLA ORELLI:**

What I can see from my practice is that intermediary agreements, which may or may not be meant to serve corruptive practices, often include representation on warranties to the effect that the intermediary represents and warrants that he will not use his efforts for corruption or similar purposes. This seems to be a very good platform for the principal to deny the lack of knowledge, and you are telling me that with regard to intention to fraud this would work?

**CHRISTOPH MÜLLER:**

I think this would be a powerful argument for the principal to say that he did not have any knowledge of the corruption, but the content of the contract would be just one source of information, one means of interpretation. If the principal's behaviour points in another direction, then I think you could nevertheless come to the conclusion that there was some intent, or some intent of representatives of the principal, to set up a corruption scheme.

**TOBIAS ZUBERBÜHLER:**

What would we do in this situation here with the main contract, as arbitrators, if none of the parties actually wants to raise any challenge to the main contract, but we feel that there are enough red flags around that we should not support the claim by the parties?

Do you see any legal basis in that situation to reject the claim as a tribunal?

**CHRISTOPH MÜLLER:**

Do you mean a claim for performance of the main contract without any allegation of error, fraud or corruption?

**TOBIAS ZUBERBÜHLER:**

Correct. Very often, both parties have unclean hands, and they do not want to even raise an issue.

**NIKOLAUS PITKOWITZ:**

I think this addresses a very sensitive and important question in a scenario where both parties try to cover up something, and the arbitral tribunal finds that there is corruption, whether the arbitral tribunal should also close its eyes and ears and say I will look on the other side. My personal view is it must not and it cannot. I think as an arbitrator, we would be otherwise concerned about being a tool used to facilitate a corrupt transaction. I am sure there are different views, but my view is that if there is something that needs to be actively addressed by the arbitral tribunal, it needs to be brought to the attention of the parties and given the opportunity to also address it if there is such a concern.

**MARIELLA ORELLI:**

That is an interesting question, but I should say that is the topic of panel 3.

**HANS VAN HOUTTE:**

I am not so sure that all legal cultures have as strict a view on the applicable law as Professor Müller, probably from the Swiss point of view. I think in many legal cultures, corruption could be a matter of international public policy, transnational public policy. The fact many countries have signed the Convention on Corruption indicates that it is a more common shared value and it is not only restricted to some specific countries.

I have two questions. The first one is we are focusing on corruption vis-à-vis states because that is what happens very often, investment arbitrations especially, but corruption can also happen in commercial transactions. If I understand Professor Müller correctly, saying those arguments about fraud could also be invoked when a contract has been concluded because of the corruption of one of the underlings in the company. Of course, you could say the problem is not as crucial because it is not public tax money, or the company should be responsible for the people he hires in order to manage the contracts. My first question is: to which extent can we project what we say here to commercial contracts?

The second question, causality: should the claimant of corruption also be obliged to prove to some extent that the corruption indeed had an impact on the conclusion of the contract? In fact, many people pretend they can influence transactions, but maybe they do not do so.

**CHRISTOPH MÜLLER:**

First, a comment to your introductory comment. I totally agree with you as far as, as I said at the beginning, outright bribery is concerned. I think with regard to the use of intermediary agreements, the consensus among international public policy is less evident, and this is why conflicts of law issues only for intermediary agreements might arise.

As to your first question, yes, I think it is absolutely transposable to commercial contracts. I made the example with the government, but the question of error and fraud to invalidate the contract applies in exactly the same way to purely private intermediary agreements.

The second question, of course, is one of the big obstacles: the proof of causation. As you know, certain jurisdictions, such as French and Belgian and other laws, are able to lower the standard of proof by using the 'loss of chance' doctrine, which often applies in disputes with respect to tenders because it is very difficult to prove that you would have obtained as a second the main contract if the first did not have it thanks to corruption. This would help to establish at least some damage even though you cannot really prove that you would have had another contract, or would even have a contract, without corruption.

Unfortunately, under Swiss law which is on this point under the influence of German law, we do not have the 'loss of chance doctrine', which is a very elegant way of dealing with the problem.

**MARIELLA ORELLI:**

Thank you for these interesting thoughts and contributions. I think it is time for Andrea Menaker to take the floor.

# Investment Arbitration Specific Issues

*Andrea Menaker*

**ANDREA MENAKER:**

Thank you also to ASA, the organisers, for having asked me to come here today. I was asked to speak about some of these issues that my co-panellists have discussed, specifically in the context of investment arbitration.

I preface these remarks by saying there are way more similarities than differences when speaking about corruption in arbitration when talking about investment arbitration as opposed to commercial arbitration, and you will see a lot of cross-fertilisation in the two systems. You see that throughout by the ways that the issues are analysed by both the parties and then by the arbitrators themselves and their awards.

Not surprisingly, in the early investment arbitration cases where corruption first arose, you see citations to Lagergren's ICC case and others that were public and vice versa. Notwithstanding that, given my task at hand, I came up with four issues where I thought there were some distinctions to be drawn between commercial and investment arbitration.

The first is considerations made in deciding to raise a corruption defence. In my view, there is more at stake for a state in an investment arbitration in deciding to raise a defence of corruption than there is as compared to a private party in a commercial arbitration.

The reason why I came to this conclusion is that, in a commercial arbitration, a party seeking to void a contract on the grounds of corruption can always raise the corruption defence and blame the illegal conduct on a rogue employee. Even if it turns out that the corruption was directed or condoned by high-level management, once that corruption has been discovered, the board of the company inevitably will instigate an investigation and almost inevitably will insist on the dismissal of those involved in the corruption or those who condoned the corruption of the company even if they are high-level management.

In the context of investor-state arbitration, however, if what we are talking about is a low-level payment to a low-level official, that is unlikely to be raised as a defence to the claim itself because there is probably not enough at stake there; you do not have the causality issues and such.

When you see these defences being raised, it is typically a larger amount, but more importantly, a high-level government official, either current or former high-level government official, that raises the stakes on the state and counsel, which is not ultimately responsible for determining whether or not to raise this defence because once raised, it can reflect very poorly on the entire government. There will be political calculations required to determine whether or not the government wants to implicate particularly current but also former high-level government officials. Whereas for the company, the ramifications can be great, and in some of these big corruption cases, you have seen even bankruptcy but still a whole different realm from the collapse of a state or a change of government in a state.

I think some of the implications for that are that you will see in the investor-state context more instances where the tribunal is faced with the question presented by one of the most recent questionnaires where they will be faced with the task of deciding whether to raise the issue of corruption *sua sponte* or not because it is not raised by the state in a case.

This also has implications because it can reflect on whether the state decides to prosecute the wrongdoers, and the bribe recipients in particular, and what implications that has on the State's defence of bribery or corruption. In some cases, the state may decide that it will go ahead and raise the defence, but nevertheless, these same concerns will prevent it from going the further step and prosecuting the recipients of the bribe.

When that happens, you often see in investment arbitration cases the claimant resisting the defence by pointing to the lack of prosecution. In a commercial case, when there is a lack of prosecution that can be explained in one of two ways: either you can say the evidence is not great enough to warrant a prosecution and so, therefore, tribunal you should also find there is no corruption here; or also clearly whether or not a state determines to prosecute is not within the hands of the commercial company so there is not much they can do about it. It is very different if you are before a tribunal and you are a state, and you are raising a corruption defence, and then you are asked if this happened, why are you not simultaneously prosecuting these government employees.

Several tribunals have been faced with this. I think it is an issue that is not going away, but, thus far in the jurisprudence, it has not been determinative or has not been a reason given by a tribunal to necessarily reject the corruption defence.

You are aware of the *World Duty Free v. Kenya* case where the former President of Kenya was implicated in the bribery scheme, and Kenya had not prosecuted that former President and that was raised. The tribunal found it troubling but nevertheless dismissed the claim.

I do not know how many of you may have been at ICA – not the past one but the congress before – where one of the counsels for Kenya really gave some interesting remarks there and discussed the fact that the Kenyan government felt that it could not prosecute because the threat of civil strife, and maybe even civil war, was so great, that the former president still had a number of loyalists and the risk would have been too great for the government to do that. That was something that was taken into account by the tribunal.

You had the same thing in *Metal-Tech v. Uzbekistan,* where I represented the respondent, and we defeated the claim on the grounds of corruption. There the bribe giver was incarcerated, albeit on different charges. The issue of corruption was just discovered during the course of the arbitration, and that implicated a former Prime Minister, but he was not prosecuted.

There were similar political sensitivities to doing that, although not in power at that time. His party, so to speak, was still in power, and that was just a very difficult political situation and was again noted by the tribunal, but given the evidence of corruption, it did not prevent the tribunal from finding corruption and dismissing the case.

The second related issue is really the dual role of the state as the prosecutor in a national court case and also the respondent in the arbitration. This is something that you also do not see in the commercial context because the host state, of course, has an obligation to prosecute corruption, and the host state cannot stop a criminal investigation just because there has been an investment arbitration filed against it.

Likewise, the investor claimant ought not to be able to stop a corruption investigation or prosecution simply by filing an arbitration claim. I think everyone agrees on those two basic tenets.

However, the State's dual role is somewhat unique because it is seeking to benefit from the outcome of a case in its national court that it is prosecuting. That places it in a much different position in the arbitration than a commercial actor, which may be the subject of criminal proceedings in the host state but which has no control over those proceedings as it is not a party or it is not the prosecuting party. There is this tension that often arises in investment arbitration cases between using the state's prosecutorial powers in order for it to comply with its domestic and international obligations to combat corruption and then has the added benefit of perhaps discovering the truth which can be used in the arbitration as well, and the potential abuse of the state's prosecutorial powers that may be used to inhibit the claimant from pursuing its claim in investment arbitration or gaining an unfair advantage in the investment arbitration.

Tribunals have really been faced with balancing these competing interests. What they have done is to try to ensure that they are not trampling on the state's sovereign right to prosecute crimes that occur, at the same time preserving the claimant's ability to bring its arbitration claim and preventing abuse by the state given its dual role.

How has this been done? The first is that almost uniformly, tribunals have recognised the state's sovereign right to prosecute crimes and have refused to issue stays or orders ordering the state to suspend criminal proceedings that are ongoing at the same time that the arbitration is ongoing.

They have imposed some limitations. In *Libananco v. Turkey,* there was an ongoing criminal investigation, and during the course of that investigation, there was wiretapping, which was lawful pursuant to the state's laws. They uncovered a lot of evidence, but they also uncovered some things that would give the state an unfair advantage in the arbitration, such as discussions between the lawyers and the claimant in the arbitration. That was obviously very worrisome.

The tribunal issued interim orders, really creating a wall between the state officials that were working on the arbitration and those that were working on the criminal investigation, and they could not share information with one another. The information that was gathered for the criminal prosecution could not be introduced into the arbitration, so they really needed to keep those things separate.

Similarly, on the other hand, I have been on the other end of that representing the Philippines in the Fraport case. There, evidence of illegality came to light during the course of the arbitration. The Philippines was prevented from sharing that evidence with the government, with their own host state government, other than the people that were involved in the arbitration itself.

This had implications later on when the claimant, for instance, had argued given that there were Congressional investigations ongoing in the Philippines, as well as several court cases dealing with the transaction at issue, they found some problems with the contract but not the illegality that we were claiming in the arbitration. The claimant said 'There are all these investigations and all these court cases in the Philippines; they did not find this illegality; it is not there. You should not find it in the arbitration.'

The tribunal's response to that was they did not have the evidence that we have before us, so the Philippines is not estopped from raising this defence here. In fact, they found in our favour on that defence and said we cannot blame the Philippines for not having reached the same conclusions because they were precluded from gaining access to this evidence.

Similarly, I am involved in a current arbitration where again, evidence that has come to light during the course of the arbitration may be shared only with the government officials who are involved in the arbitration but not more broadly with the state. To the extent that there are, or might be, prosecutions or investigations, at least while the arbitration is ongoing, this sharing of information is not permitted.

One exception to the statement that I made earlier about tribunals not suspending criminal proceedings is one that you are probably aware of in *Kaborax v. Bolivia* (check), where there is a very particular factual situation, but the tribunal had actually concluded that the criminal proceedings in Bolivia were actually instigated in response to the claimant's filing the arbitration claims, sort of in retaliation for having done that.

That tribunal actually issued an interim order provisional measure directing Bolivia to refrain from initiating any other criminal proceedings and suspending the current proceedings. Bolivia did not comply with that provisional order, they continued, but nevertheless, several years later, the tribunal in its award, where it did find that Bolivia had admitted a breach of the treaty, found that Bolivia's refusal to comply with the order did not amount to a breach of their duty to arbitrate in good faith because it had not been shown that the arbitral procedure or the integrity of the proceedings had been violated or that any prejudice had really materialised to the claimant in relation to their ability to prosecute their claim or with respect to their ability to gain access to witnesses and the like.

I think I may keep you in suspense as to the last two issues given the time. Perhaps I will end here so I can leave a little time for questions.

**MARIELLA ORELLI:**

Thank you for sharing your insights on investment arbitration. You mentioned the considerations for a state to raise the corruption defence, the illegality defence based on corruption. What about the considerations for an investor when defending against allegations of corruption raised by the state? Connected with that, how far can counsel go in supporting potential efforts by the clients to brush all these matters under the carpet?

**ANDREA MENAKER:**

I think the claimant generally is not raising corruption as a defence. In certain circumstances, I have seen the claimant raise the issue but in support of its claim. That primarily has arisen where the claimant has made allegations that a bribe was solicited from it and that it refused to pay the bribe and, therefore, they did not get the contract or that then retaliated against them by doing something to their investment and giving it to somebody else.

I have seen that claim raised in two cases; both happened to fail for lack of evidence. The tribunal found it was not supported. I do think if there is sufficient evidence, a claimant could raise that, and that, in and of itself, would constitute a breach of probably the fair and equitable treatment standard that is present in most investment treaties. To retaliate or to harm an investment for its refusal to pay bribes is obviously a violation of that treaty obligation.

With respect to your second question, as counsel, you can advise your client and, of course, whoever you are representing, you want to make the best arguments for them so from a legal perspective, if you feel that there is evidence that can support a defence you want to make it, but ultimately that is going to be a decision the client has to make. You might be in a position to raise a defence and yet not point the finger at a recipient, but sometimes that is not really going to work, depending on the facts. Ultimately, that is not a decision that you can make unilaterally without your client.

**MARIELLA ORELLI:**

What do you do if you find out in preparing for an arbitration that the investor paid a bribe to state officials or people whose conduct is attributable to the state? Would you tell the client not to build a case because the investment is tainted, or how do you deal with it?

**ANDREA MENAKER:**

If I was representing a claimant who I found out had bribed, yes, I would tell them that is bad, that is corruption, a violation, unlawful, and that likely will result in the dismissal of your claim, and that is not a good way to go forward.

**SILJA SCHAFFSTEIN:**

Could you comment on the tension that exists between the fact that it is well accepted that a claim that is tainted with corruption will not pass, the tribunal will dismiss it usually on jurisdiction? However, are we not incentivising governments to continue their corrupt practices? It is an unsatisfactory result because, yes, the claimant has been corrupted but so has the state.

**ANDREA MENAKER:**

In some respects, it is unsatisfactory because of what you say, but I think that analogy breaks down in this context because, ultimately, the state is not benefiting from the corruption. The state is being harmed by corruption. You have an official who has taken some money, and that act really, in my view, ought not to be attributable to the state. The state itself is not benefiting from that money, and certainly, the state is a reflection, or they are representing the populace of that country. The state's citizenry is certainly not benefiting from that corruption; they are being harmed by it.

That I think initially is my first response.

Second, as a practical matter, yes, the state may benefit in having this one claim dismissed but ultimately if a state is a repeat player in investment arbitrations and consistently has claims defeated on the grounds of corruption and it becomes known, as Kate was saying, as a country where corruption is really endemic, I think that hurts their investment prospects.

The purpose of these treaties is to promote and also to protect investments, but it is the promotion of investments as well. If it is going to harm their ability to attract investment into the country, if they think that the only way you can get in there is to pay bribes, then your investments are going to lose the protection of those investment treaties.

It is a two-way street for the states as well, and I think they recognise this. When raising the defence, they also want to send a signal to the world that they are open to clean investment and they will protect that investment, and that becomes increasingly difficult if they are enmeshed in these corruption scandals.

**MARIELLA ORELLI:**

In *Duty Free*, I think some academic writers would take the view that states in which the level of corruption is very high, that is, in which corruption is endemic, should be estopped from raising the illegality issue as a defence. What is your view about that?

**ANDREA MENAKER:**

I do not believe so. I would look to Mark Pieth, wherever he is right now. Certainly, it is not only domestically unlawful but internationally unlawful. I do not think a valid defence is 'Well, everyone does it.' If you go down that route, nothing will change.

It is in the international community's interest to stamp out corruption to the extent we can and to move towards that goal. I think the only way to do that is really to hold firm to the idea that these transactions that are corrupt are not to be validated, and you let the chips fall where they may and hope that changes future behaviour; otherwise, you are just giving in to the corruption, and nothing will change.

**MARIELLA ORELLI:**

The organisers are telling me that I should close the session. Thank you for this contribution. It was very interesting.

# Panel 3: The Impact of Alleged or Demonstrated Corruption on the Arbitral Process

*Moderated by Rikard Wikström-Hermansen*

**ANDREA MEIER:**

I am very happy to introduce Panel 3 and particularly the moderator, Rikard Wikström-Hermansen, a Stockholm-based partner at Roschier. He focuses on Swedish and international commercial arbitration and Swedish court proceedings. Rikard is recognised as one of the leading experts in dispute resolution and arbitration in Sweden, and clients say that Rikard is 'extremely reliable and creative, a very experienced lawyer with a good sense of strategy and tremendous under pressure', so the pressure is on!

**RIKARD WIKSTRÖM-HERMANSEN:**

Thank you for that fantastic introduction. Thank you to ASA for inviting me and for organising this, and for the wonderful dinner last night. It was my first time ever trying the Double Creme Gruyère. I am not a dessert fan, but I ate it all. I love that we have a stenographer and that it is on record!

On that note, however, because of some conversations I had during lunch now, I want to emphasise to everyone in the audience that the fact that we are taking this up on the transcript, please do not let that stop you from raising questions and comments. You are in control of the transcript afterwards and can delete it. I heard some very interesting comments, so please share.

I have the pleasure of moderating this panel. We have fantastic panellists. We have Kate Davies on my left, a partner in Allen & Overy's International Arbitration Group in London with extensive experience in both commercial and investment treaty arbitration and really one of the stars of my generation in international arbitration. She is not only based in London but proudly hails from the city, a city which – and here I quote Kate – 'voted overwhelming to stay in the EU', so do not blame Kate or London.

The overall topic of Panel 3 is the impact of alleged or demonstrated corruption on the arbitral process. Our three panellists will each have a presentation, and we will have discussions after each.

Kate's presentation will be followed by Professor Pierre Mayer's presentation. He needs not much introduction. As many of you know, he is an independent arbitrator based in Paris. I think it is very impressive that you were a professor for almost thirty years at the University of Paris I, teaching both international arbitration and private international law, where you are also the Professor Emeritus since 2012.

When I asked Pierre if there was something particular I should mention about him, he replied that 'One thing that distinguishes me from most of the other speakers is that I was born in Geneva.'

Last but not least, we have, on my right, Anne-Catherine Hahn, a partner at Baker McKenzie's Zurich office. She hails from the other Protestant region of Switzerland or works there at least and has stated that according to some, it competes with Geneva not only as a place of arbitration but also in terms of sobriety!

Anne-Catherine Hahn is focused on commercial arbitration. She has for many years lectured at the University of Fribourg, where she also has her doctorate.

That is our fantastic talent. I give the floor to Kate, who will address the issue: if corruption taints the process itself: corrupt arbitrators, experts and witnesses.

# If Corruption Taints the Process Itself: Corrupt Arbitrators, Experts and Witnesses

*Kate Davies*

**KATE DAVIES:**

I am going to stay seated for my presentation because experience tells me that I will be vertically challenged if I stand up against that lectern and the laptop. I only discovered this in the last year because I broke my ankle in three places last May – so I have sympathy with the Ernst & Young gentleman earlier who was here with apparently two broken knees – and I had to wear flat shoes in the office for the best part of ten months. Everybody remarked upon the fact, 'Kate, you are really short.' I am going to stay seated because I can at least pretend I am a bit taller!

Thank you for that introduction and to ASA for inviting me here today. I am going to cover three topics in fairly brief order. I will only be able to touch upon the issues. I am going to start by defining what I mean by corruption. We had a whole panel on that this morning, but I want to come back to that because it is an important framework for what it is that I am then going to talk about. I will then talk about the consequences of corruption within the arbitral process itself and then the consequences of that kind of corruption beyond the arbitral framework.

Before I do that I want to tell you about a dream. It is not my dream; it is a dream that a client of mine, who is the general counsel of ethics and compliance at a very large oil major, told me about last week. It goes as follows: in her dream, she is approaching a ticket machine where you slot money into the ticket machine and take out a ticket. If you have put in too much change, you get the change out at the bottom. She walks up to the machine to get her ticket, and she puts her hand in the change slot at the bottom, and she discovers a whole load of change. She pockets the change – it does not belong to anybody – takes a ticket, and off she goes.

In the next stage of her dream, she walks up to the ticket machine, which is wide open, and there are stacks of cash sitting inside the ticket machine and two men – not necessarily specifically men, but they happen to be two men in her dream – come up to the ticket machine, grab the cash and run away. She walks over to the officials who are manning the ticket office and says, 'You need to stop those two guys; they have run away with stacks of cash', but nothing happens.

Then in her dream, she says to herself, 'Hang on a second. I am criticising the men for stealing the cash and criticising the officials for not doing anything about it, but what about me? I took the change. Am I any better than they are?'

The reason that story struck me at the time in the context of what I am talking about today is because we spend a lot of time talking about corruption in arbitration, and we are talking about corruption that happens over there; it is somebody else involved in the corruption.

The topic of my presentation is slightly more uncomfortable because perhaps it does touch us. We all have to look inwards and ask ourselves if we are any better because we have taken the change in the bottom of the slot machine.

What do I mean by corruption in that context? There is a useful English law definition of corruption which I think captures very nicely what it is that I mean by corruption. It is causing someone to transfer their loyalty away from their duty and towards the corrupter. When you understand corruption in that context, you understand that it is something more than, in the context of corruption within the arbitral process, a claimant saying to an arbitrator, 'I will give you 10% of my award if you find in my favour and award me X in damages.'

That may sound incredibly shocking to everybody in this room, and we can all sit here and say, 'I would never do that. I would never take the cash from the ticket machine', but if you are to believe Stephen Vassilev's (check) report in 2016 of him overhearing precisely that boast being made by the arbitrator concerned, it happens in arbitration.

That is an obvious example of somebody transferring their loyalty from their duty of impartiality and independence to the parties and the process away from that duty and towards the corrupt claimant offering the money.

There are less obvious examples. What about the claimant, or the claimant's counsel, who takes the arbitrator out for coffee and says over the course of that coffee, 'I really like appointing you as an arbitrator. I have had a really good experience, and if I continue to have that good experience, then I will continue to appoint you in other arbitrations.' Does that qualify as corruption? Under some definitions, including the English definition of corruption, that would qualify as a bribe because you are offering to transfer the arbitrator's loyalty from his duty towards the claimant.

A third example does not involve the claimant and the arbitrator; I move to the parties now. Let us say the finance director of a company is caused by that company to give evidence in the context of an arbitration about the accounts of that company in support of a claim for damages.

That account is false, and not only is the account that he gives verbally and his witness statement false, but he also produces false statements of account to support his evidence which is then relied upon by the expert in the arbitration.

That is broader than the narrow sense of what we understand of corruption, it is more fraud, but I am going to use that as well as an example when I come to talk about the consequences of these kinds of acts.

That is what I mean by corruption: something overt and direct but also much more subtle, and I think it is important to have that in mind when thinking about corruption.

What are the consequences of any one of those three examples happening within the arbitration? In a sense, this is the easy bit, and everyone might think it is really obvious. The first thing you do as the respondent who uncovers – if you are lucky enough to uncover this kind of corruption – you would challenge the arbitrator, to which you might say, 'Are not arbitrators immune from liability?' Yes, but only so far.

Certainly, under the English Arbitration Act, section 29, which confers judicial-style immunity on arbitrators, is limited to good faith discharge of duties. It specifically does not apply to duties discharged in bad faith. There is a judicial commentary on what bad faith means in that context, and almost unquestionably, although there is no case law on this, it would include an arbitrator who accepts a bribe in the form that I described earlier, certainly the first one, the overt one. Arbitral immunity is no answer to a challenge to the arbitrator; so far, so good.

What about challenging the award?

Again, it might seem obvious if the claimant has bribed the arbitrator or if the finance director has, on behalf of the company, given false evidence on the basis of false accounts. Surely you would be able to argue, under section 62.2(g) of the English Arbitration Act and its equivalent under other jurisdictions, that the award was obtained by fraud.

In the case of the bribe of the arbitrator by the party or the party's counsel, that is probably obviously right. You would be able to challenge the award on that basis.

On the second basis where it is the finance director of the company, again the position is probably obviously yes, you would be able to challenge the award on that basis because the award has been obtained by the fraud of the party and there is an English case law that says the finance director or a senior official or employee of the company who gives false evidence on the company's behalf in order to pervert the award that would be obtained by the fraud of the party.

Let us say it was not the finance director. Let us say it is a third party who is persuaded by the company to give that evidence and the evidence is false, and it is on the basis of that evidence that at least some part of the award is obtained. Certainly, under English case law, it is not obvious that you would be able to challenge the award under section 68.2(g) because it would be arguable, at least by the party perpetrating the corrupt act and obtaining false evidence, that that was not obtained by the party because the witness in question was employed by somebody else.

What you begin to uncover when you look into this is actually a fairly surprising approach, certainly of the English courts, to corruption and the public policy exception. I think the direction, or at least the weight, at the moment of English case law tends to be in favour of the public policy of enforcing an arbitral award over – in other words; it has greater value – than the public policy of not allowing corrupt acts or people who engage in corruption to benefit from those acts. That is perhaps surprising and is probably something that I hope will change and certainly needs to change in my own personal view.

That is challenging the arbitrator and challenging the award. What if you do not discover the corruption or the false evidence by which the award has been obtained until you get to the enforcement stage? Obviously, you might say you would be able to resist enforcement of the award again under the fraud exception under the New York Convention.

There was an interesting case in the English High Court that then went to the English Court of Appeal a couple of years ago, *Stati v. Republic of Kazakhstan*, which involved an underlying energy charter treaty claim, and the arbitration had its seat in Sweden. The claimants in that case prevailed in the arbitration. They got the award of USD 500 million, USD 199 million of which related to the valuation of a liquid petroleum plant that had been confiscated by Kazakhstan and in respect of which they recovered USD 199 million worth of damages.

The state challenged the award at the seat on the basis that it was procured by fraud, and that challenge was not upheld by the Swedish court. There were then enforcement proceedings in the US and a disclosure application in the US.

It was in the course of the disclosure application that evidence came to light, which the state managed to obtain, to suggest that the valuation of USD 199 million was indeed based on evidence that had been fraudulently obtained, so it was false evidence.

The claimants then sought to enforce the award in London, and that is where the story begins. The state, perhaps not surprisingly, sought to resist enforcement of the award on the basis that it had been obtained by fraud, at which point the claimant sought to discontinue the proceedings and said, 'It is okay; we do not need to enforce our award in London. We undertake not to enforce the award in London. We can enforce it elsewhere.'

The question before the Court of Appeal was whether, as the state argued, the court was nevertheless required to continue to hear the fraud allegation because it was, in effect, a fraud on the processes of the English court.

The judge at first instance said yes; they were required to go ahead and hear the claim of the fraud because it was a fraud on the court's processes, but the Court of Appeal disagreed.

They disagreed because the only basis on which the application had come before the court was for enforcement of the award. There was not a self-standing application in relation to the fraud. The fraud only arose in the context of resisting enforcement and because there was no fraud on the court's processes because there was no fraud concerned in the actual application that was made for enforcement. The fraud occurred outside of the application and within the four corners of the arbitration.

Perhaps one might say rather unsatisfactorily what happens to have been at least prima facie evidence of fraud, at least evidence that was sufficient to cause the claimant in that case to file a motion of discontinuance in respect of the enforcement, never saw the light of day and they have since then been able to enforce their award for half a billion dollars.

That leads to the third part of my presentation, which is the consequences outside of arbitration. I am really pleased to see here today the bringing together of the arbitration world and the white-collar world because I, for better or worse, have spent a lot of the last few years dealing with corruption in an arbitral context, not in the arbitral process but in an arbitration context.

My sadly overwhelming experience has been a lack of understanding in the arbitral world of the way in which the white-collar world approaches corruption and the manner in which the international community, including pursuant to the OECD Convention, has decided to treat corruption because of its deleterious effects.

If I go back to my three examples, the overt bribing of the arbitrator, the lesser bribing of the arbitrator, and the financial director who gives a false account in his evidence, all three of those are criminal offences under the English Bribery Act. They are also offences under the Theft Act, and they are also offences under the POCA Act.

There is also a focus on the FCPA, and we saw the slide earlier with all the massive fines that the FCPA has imposed. Maxi asked the question: are other enforcement agencies taking a similar approach? The answer is, yes, only recently in the UK. The *Rolls Royce* case is the most recent we have. USD 450 million fine, only USD 170 million of which went to the US enforcement agencies. The majority of that fine was enforced through UK agencies. There is an increasing awareness within other agencies outside of the US of the importance of prosecuting these crimes, and like the FCPA, the UK Bribery Act has an extraterritorial reach.

Let us take an example where the claimant who seeks to bribe the arbitrator is sitting in his office in New York, the arbitrator is in Paris, and they are talking about an arbitration seated in Sweden. Does any of that constitute a crime within the UK Bribery Act?

Yes, if the claimant is making that bribe on behalf of a company with a connection to the UK. They do not have to have their headquarters there, but if they have a connection to the UK, they can be caught within the Bribery Act. That is not just the person making the bribe but the person receiving the bribe. If any part of the offence is committed in the UK, it constitutes a crime.

In addition to the extraterritorial reach of the UK Bribery Act, what distinguishes bribery and corruption from fraud – and I think this is something people forget – there is no element of dishonesty in corruption. That is something often that I find difficult to persuade tribunals of when dealing with corruption. You do not have to conclude that the people who perpetrated this were dishonest or bad. The fact of making the bribe or offering an incentive to do something other than what you should be doing is sufficient to be caught within the Criminal Act.

The other point – and I will not go into this too much because I know Professor Mayer is going to be talking about this more – in terms of shifting the burden of proof, there is a piece of legislation that dates back to the First World War. It was emergency legislation that was introduced to try to stop people bribing public officials, in the context of the First World War, to gain contracts for the production of arms. The emergency legislation effectively shifted the burden of proof, once an allegation of corruption had been made, to the person who had been accused.

That legislation has sat on the English statute book for a very long time, the best part of a century, and it is only now that the law commission and the government has said it is time for that to be removed because the shifting of the burden of proof has no place in dealing with corruption. There are other ways of dealing with it. I do not want to tread on Professor Mayer's toes.

That is my whistlestop tour of corruption in the arbitral process. It is a difficult topic. It is uncomfortable for all of us, and if you believe the limited reports that you read about this, it is happening, and none of us is immune to it, and we all have to be aware of it.

**RIKARD WIKSTRÖM-HERMANSEN:**

I just wanted to follow up. You touched upon the legal consequences of the finding of corruption, and interestingly, Panel 2 had a discussion towards the end. Traditionally, arbitral tribunals have had a very binary all or nothing approach: once you find corruption, then the claim is out. Recently, there has been this trend, both in case law and commentaries, towards a more so-called proportion approach. Taking the position, as was touched upon by Panel 2, that this can encourage if you have a corrupt respondent state, they can consistently get away with the obligations under a treaty because of corruption.

In *ING v. Uzbekistan*, the tribunal stated when they considered the corruption that they were 'guided by the principle of proportionality' and found that it was required to 'balance the object of promoting economic relations by providing a stable investment framework with the harsh consequence of denying the application of the treaty in total'.

It is my understanding that the Supreme Court in the UK has also had this issue and confirmed this proportionality approach in *Patel v. Mirza*. I was curious if you have a view on proportionality or all or nothing?

**KATE DAVIES:**

I do. I think there are two parts to that: what is my view of *the Uzbekistan* decision and the approach of proportionality, and then is Supreme Court following that approach?

First, on the proportionality approach, you have to distinguish between, as earlier panels have spoken about, corruption in order to establish the investment, when you are talking about an investor-state context, then corruption in the performance of the contract. There are distinct civil consequences of that from a contractual perspective, and it is right that they are kept distinct.

As far as a general approach to proportionality goes, when dealing with corruption, I do not agree with it. The reason I do not agree with it is because I am informed by the work that I have done with my white-collar colleagues in this area where there is very little proportionality, at least as regards the initial incidence of corruption.

Where you get proportionality in the criminal sphere is in the fine and the consequences of corruption. If you are talking about corruption in the performance of the contract, yes, you might take a proportionate approach to damages, but the states who make up the OECD Convention have decided between themselves that the consequences of corruption are so severe that there should be an all or nothing approach.

I am always struck by the example of an Australian mining company who paid an AUD 4 bribe to a local official to get them to do something which they were meant to do anyway, and that triggered a whole series of investigations which resulted in a very large fine. That is because of the zero-tolerance approach to corruption taken at the state level and outside of arbitration. I am not a fan of the proportionate approach.

As for the English Supreme Court and the approach it takes, I do not think *Patel v. Mirza* is authority for the fact that the English court takes a proportionate approach to corruption. That case was an insider dealing case, and the person who paid a sum of money, on the basis of insider information to this bank to make an investment in a bank's shares, knowing those banks were going to nosedive, was seeking restitution of the money it had paid for that purpose.

It was not a corruption case at all, but the Supreme Court made a comment about corruption because corruption cases had been introduced in the context of the illegality defence. What the Supreme Court said was, 'it is not clear to me that there is any greater policy served by restituting the money back to the person who paid it in the first place who was guilty of insider trading versus leaving it with the bank who was also guilty of insider trading because they were continuing the crime'. There was a public policy balancing what was going on in that case, but I do not think they were saying there is a proportionate case.

What the Supreme Court also said in that case, which I do think is right and it is right that a distinction between the two things is that there is civil law approach to corruption and its consequences, particularly within a contractual framework, and then there are the criminal consequences. It is right that the fines and the disgorgement and all of the consequences of corruption in that context take place within the criminal sphere; that is no function of the arbitral tribunal.

**RIKARD WIKSTRÖM-HERMANSEN:**

Unless there are comments from the audience, you can save it, and I instead give the word to Professor Mayer, who will discuss the burden of proof, duty and power of arbitrators to investigate, and also the evidentiary issues and standards of proof.

# Duty and Power of Arbitrators to Investigate and Evidentiary Issues

*Pierre Mayer*

**PIERRE MAYER:**

Kate's presentation dealt with corruption in the arbitral process. I will deal with corruption related to the substance of the case, which means in practice corruption in the contract that is the subject of the arbitration. There is an allegation by a party or a suspicion by the arbitrator that either the contract was procured by corruption or the contract aims at corrupting: in the second case, the contract is between the principal and the intermediary, which we heard about earlier, and it aims at procuring by corruption another contract, for instance, an investment or a procurement contract. Of course, if corruption is proved, the contents of the award will reflect it. The tribunal will declare the contract void or will at least refuse to order that it be performed.

The question we are asking ourselves now is: what are the powers and the duties of the arbitrator in that regard.

Sometimes it is very simple. One party alleges that there has been corruption, and that party proves it beyond a reasonable doubt; pursuant to the applicable law or transnational public policy, the contract is, therefore, null and void, so the arbitrator's duty is simply to apply the law to the facts proven.

Things are generally not so simple because corruption is normally carefully hidden, and it is not so easy to prove. It also happens rather frequently that the party which refuses to perform its contractual obligation nevertheless does not dare invoke the existence of corruption.

Should the arbitrator be proactive? The answer may differ, depending on whether one party invokes corruption or both parties are silent about the existence of corruption. I will deal successively with these two situations, but before that, I would like to briefly reflect upon the general considerations from which the arbitrator derives his or her inspiration.

One very powerful consideration, to which arbitrators are extremely sensitive, is the risk that their award be set aside by the state court which exercises its control: the award infringes public policy if it orders the performance of a contract which, in fact, was obtained by corruption. Arbitrators hate seeing their award set aside. It is a question of pride. It is also a question of reputation if the judgment is made public. If they ordered the party to implement the contract, but the controlling court finds that the contract was obtained by corruption or that it was aiming at corruption, then the award will be set aside, and the fear that that happens plays a very important role.

Of course, if in a given country, courts do not exercise their control carefully and only react when the violation of public policy is flagrant, or if courts do not have the power to review the facts and the evidence, then the risk of annulment is rather low and the incentive to establish the truth and to sanction corruption disappears.

Independently from that fear, two opposing considerations may come into play. Some arbitrators are sensitive to the first and others to the second.

The first consideration is: this is the parties' case, I must not interfere. There might indeed be corruption, there are some red flags, but no party has brought decisive evidence; therefore, corruption is not proven. I do not have to go further. *Pacta sunt servanda*, the contract must be performed. That is one consideration.

The second, opposite, consideration is: corruption is immoral; it may ruin the economy of a country; it is an evil, as we have heard from several persons, in particular Mark Pieth and Thomas Werlen, this morning. There are sacred interests involved. Although I, the arbitrator, am sitting in a private dispute about a private contract, the effect of my award will go beyond the interests of the parties. As a citizen, which I do not cease to be just because I am an arbitrator – I am still a citizen – I must do my best to render an award that does not infringe public policy, such an important public policy.

I am personally persuaded more by the second consideration than by the first. However, it is a purely subjective choice. There is no rule of law that decides what I must do. Arbitrators are free. There are two trends; I follow the second, and others follow the first.

In light of this, let me address the first situation, which is the one in which one party, generally the respondent, argues that the contract is unlawful because it was obtained by corruption or aims at corruption. I will deal with that situation rather briefly and with the second situation more at length.

*In the first situation*, corruption is alleged by one party, but that party fails to convince the tribunal completely. The proof is not there. There are some red flags. Most arbitrators will simply say to that party: 'You have the burden of proof; you say that there is corruption, prove it; if you do not prove it, then no corruption exists, and I will order that the contract be performed.'

Some arbitrators, however, will use their power of investigation in order to find out the truth. As an example of that attitude, I will quote the famous *Metal-Tech / Uzbekistan* ICSID award rendered by a tribunal chaired by Gabrielle Kaufmann-Kohler.

The state was arguing that the tribunal lacked jurisdiction because the approval of the investment by the state had been obtained by corruption. However, the state was not bringing sufficient evidence. The tribunal decided to go further; I quote the award:

'The payment of substantial sums having been admitted, the tribunal considered it its duty to inquire about the reasons for such payments.' In the exercise of its ex officio powers, the tribunal, therefore, invited the parties, in Procedural Order No. 7, to provide that information, and in Procedural Order No. 10, the tribunal once again exercised its ex officio powers to call for additional testimony and evidence.

Does this go too far? Personally, I do not think so.

What, now, if no party alleges that there has been corruption although the facts inevitably raise a suspicion? That is the *second situation.*

It raises two problems: first, does the arbitrator have the power to raise the issue of corruption ex officio? Second, when is it appropriate to raise the question, is there even a duty in some cases?

*As to the power*, the situation is the following: it appears from the facts that have been disclosed that corruption is almost certain, or even absolutely certain; however, the parties do not say a word about it. They do not answer the tribunal's questions which the tribunal asks about it, or they even tell the arbitrator: 'Forget about this issue of corruption you are mentioning; it is not part of the mission we entrust to you. Your mission is restrained to the interpretation and to the performance of the contract.' Can the arbitrator ignore this and say: 'No. I go further, and I annul the contract, or at least I refuse to order the performance?'

In my opinion - which can be discussed - the answer is in the negative. The mission of the arbitrator is that which is given to him by the parties. He cannot extend it by his own will. In addition, if he took the position: 'You tell me not to deal with this issue of corruption but I will, I consider that I have the duty to do it', then the parties, since they agree on this point, will simply terminate his mission. I do not think that is the right approach.

Nevertheless, the arbitrator does not want to order the performance of an obligation that results from a contract visibly, or very likely, tainted by corruption. I see only one possibility, which is to refuse to adjudicate the case.

On what grounds? This morning a certain famous award was mentioned, rendered in 1963 by a Swedish judge, Judge Lagergren, acting as a sole arbitrator. Incidentally, thirty years after this award was rendered, another Swede, Gillis Wetter, came into possession of the award, which had not been published. He read it and wrote an article describing precisely what the situation had been.

Contrary to what has sometimes been said, the foundation of Judge Lagergren's refusal to adjudicate the case is not that he thought that issues of corruption are not for arbitrators. Judge Lagergren felt very strongly that there was corruption, but it was not really proven. He asked for explanations from the parties, but they refused to answer. Then, he said: 'In these conditions, I cannot deal with the request to order performance of the contract. What can I do? I can only say that I have no jurisdiction.'

Generally, this award is criticised. I think it can be approved because the mission that the parties wanted to entrust to Judge Lagergren might have forced him to order the performance of a contract which, in his opinion, had almost certainly been obtained by corruption.

What was, technically, the ground for lack of jurisdiction? The arbitration had been brought on the basis of a '*compromis*' (an arbitration agreement, not a clause in the contract). This *compromis* was unlawful because it would have obliged the arbitrator to order the performance of the contract without being able to object that he felt there had been corruption. I think the truncated mission conferred by the arbitration agreement was in itself contrary to public policy because it could lead to that result, hence the lack of jurisdiction.

That brings me to the second question: *is there a duty*, not a mere power, to raise the issue of corruption? Judge Lagergren clearly felt he had a duty because he was practically convinced that there was corruption, and the refusal to answer his questions only confirmed that.

In most cases, there are only some red flags, and the arbitrator suspects that there was corruption, but it is not certain that there was. Should he investigate, ask questions to the parties? Important authors have answered in the negative. Redfern and Hunter: 'It is not the duty of an arbitral tribunal to assume an inquisitorial role and to search officially for evidence of corruption when none is alleged.' Going even further, Alexis Mourre: 'Arbitrators should not turn themselves into investigators, policemen or prosecutors. The primary role of an arbitrator is to enforce the contract and not to defend public policy.'

I am not convinced at all by these statements: where it appears that a violation of the public policy would very likely result from the enforcement of the contract, the arbitrator must go further and ask questions to the parties.

Of course, it all depends on the seriousness of the suspicion, and that is a very difficult point. Just because there is a faint flavour of corruption but nothing really specific, is it justified to inquire further? Suppose the suspicion arises only because corruption is endemic in the country, but there is nothing else; am I allowed to ask questions to the parties and go further? Where is the threshold?

That is a difficult question, and since I am at the end of the time allocated for my presentation, I will be waiting for a question from the Chairman to try to give an answer.

**RIKARD WIKSTRÖM-HERMANSEN:**

We will see if that question is put to you. I was curious. I get the impression, Kate, that you strongly afford a duty for arbitrators to investigate, and Pierre just made the case, and underlying those quotes is also the argument that actually, by doing that, you are interfering with the fundamental principle of equal treatment. I am hoping that you will take the opposite position here on duty.

**ANNE-CATHERINE HAHN:**

I am not sure I take the opposite position. What I would say is that I would expect the evidence to be relevant to the outcome of the case. Cases involving allegations of bribery can be very messy, and sometimes facts are invoked which relate to a party's overall background and history or to conduct which may or may not be relevant for the case and which needs to be carefully assessed by the tribunal.

There also can be uncertainties or at least diverging views on the legal rules.

If you look, for example, at money laundering activities, you can see that the concept of predicate offence has been substantially extended in recent years to also comprise tax fraud and tax evasion. These offences can, in turn, be related to the use of slush funds for the purposes of bribery, but not necessarily so. Therefore, when drawing deductions from indicia of improper conduct, it is important to ensure that such indicia are relevant for the dispute submitted to a tribunal.

This said I would clearly support the position that indicia should be taken into account if they are relevant for the outcome of the case. Also because as an arbitrator, you have to be concerned about your own role and avoid becoming an instrument by parties who perhaps want to get an enforceable title by withholding relevant evidence from the tribunal.

If an arbitrator is put in a position where he or she is being instrumentalised to produce a 'sham award', the ultimate step may be to resign, but this obviously is a very drastic measure that should be limited to extreme situations in which both parties appear to be involved in such an abuse of the arbitration. To come to such a conclusion, arbitrators will no doubt have to try investigating the parties' positions and conduct in an independent manner and also take into account evidence from outside the proceedings, but again.

**RIKARD WIKSTRÖM-HERMANSEN:**

A cautious approach but still with a duty to investigate. That leads us to the question, Pierre Mayer, if I may ask you: you have a situation the example you were alluding to, there are no arguments from either party of corruption. Could you, from a practical perspective, give examples of where you think it triggers the ex officio *sua sponte* obligation to ask questions?

**PIERRE MAYER:**

I will rather give you an example in which it does not trigger; it is simpler. Suppose that the reason for the suspicion is only that in the state there is endemic corruption, and so it is unlikely that any contract of great importance, for instance, a contract for the exploration and exploitation of an iron ore mountain or an oilfield, can be obtained without corruption. That, for me, is not sufficient. Why? After all, one could say that the balance of probability – if it is the correct standard – is rather that there has been corruption. But that is not enough, and not even enough to ask questions because it is a situation in which the answers will not help you. You will ask: 'Is there not corruption in this case?' and both parties will say: 'Absolutely not, it is shocking to say that', and you will not have made any progress.

You can only start asking questions when there is a *specific point*, a fact, which really legitimately raises suspicion; you may ask the parties to elaborate on that fact. If you see that the parties do not want to answer, or their answer is clearly elusive, then you have additional evidence by their attitude that there was corruption; it may still be insufficient, but at least you will have improved your understanding of the situation. In Lagergren's case, there was enough evidence to justify the refusal to adjudicate the case.

My answer is, therefore: if you think that by asking questions, your understanding of the situation will progress, notwithstanding the reticence of the parties, then you can ask questions. If there is no hope that you will get anything, do not.

**RIKARD WIKSTRÖM-HERMANSEN:**

On the burden of proof, it is such an interesting discussion, where many take the position clearly that allegations of illegality must be proven, like any other allegation, whereas others point to the fact Kate alluded to earlier how these are typical activities that are concealed. In particular, in relation to intermediary agreements, there have been discussions that there should be a reversal of the burden proof. One argument in support of that has been that it is easy for the party who is being accused of the corrupt activities to submit evidence that these intermediary payments were lawful; they were for this and this expenses, et cetera. What is your view on shifting the burden of proof?

**PIERRE MAYER:**

I think there is no shifting, and there is no reversal. That problem rests on a confusion on the notion of burden of proof. Burden of proof means two different things. First, the burden of proof commands who is going to lose, who is going to win, when there is still a doubt on a certain alleged fact. If the burden of proof rests on the claimant, and the claimant does not convince the tribunal or court, its position will not prevail. The party which has the burden of proof loses when there is still a doubt; it has the duty to convince.

That is one thing. The burden always rests on the party, which alleges the fact. You allege a fact; you have to prove it. If you do not convince the tribunal that the fact exists, the fact will be considered non-existent.

The second meaning, the second notion of burden of proof – and it is a pity that there is only one expression to describe both concepts – is the burden of bringing evidence, bringing documents, witness statements, *et cetera*. That is a completely different question, and that burden rests on both parties. Both parties have an interest in bringing evidence. The one which alleges that there is corruption will bring evidence to that effect, and the party which denies that there was corruption if it has the possibility to bring evidence to that effect, will do it spontaneously. It will not wait until the alleging party has brought some evidence to bring its own counterevidence. Both parties will bring their evidence. There is no shifting of that burden. It rests on both parties because each of them wants to win.

**RIKARD WIKSTRÖM-HERMANSEN:**

That is interesting. Michael Hwang and Kevin Lim have written an article, published on the ICA website, and they, like you, clearly side against the shifting of the burden of proof, but then they state that the solution could be that if the alleging party, the party that alleges corrupt activities, can submit prima facie evidence, or if there is prima facie evidence of corrupt activities and the party that is being accused of corrupt activities does not submit proof, that you can draw adverse inferences.

You mentioned a document production order. Funnily, I had a conversation with Anna Noël at the break where we discussed this. My question is, and I have a slight concern with this: drawing adverse inferences is that not really reversing the burden of proof? I would be interested to hear if you were drawing adverse inferences and, if so, in which cases?

**PIERRE MAYER:**

I think I would, in a context in which there is already some evidence that there has been corruption. Take, for instance, the case of an intermediary which claims its fees: 5% of the amount of the main contract with the principal. The other party says: 'The aim of this contract was to corrupt officials in the country; I request you, if you deny it, to tell me what work you have done and to prove it.' Can really the other party, the intermediary, say: 'No, I do not have the burden of proof. I have nothing to say.' If it is said that, I would definitely draw adverse inferences.

**RIKARD WIKSTRÖM-HERMANSEN:**

Mindful of the time or lack of time, we look forward to hearing from Anne-Catherine Hahn on the judicial scrutiny of corruption.

# Judicial Scrutiny of Corruption-Tainted Arbitral Awards at the Setting Aside and Enforcement Stage

*Anne-Catherine Hahn*

**ANNE-CATHERINE HAHN:**

Professor Mayer mentioned that arbitral tribunals are and should be concerned about their award not being set aside or enforced. This judicial control constitutes one of the main controls on the arbitral process. Arbitration is based on a delegation of judicial powers, and ultimately the state defines the framework and the controls that give the process legitimacy. The judicial control, primarily in setting aside but indirectly also in enforcement proceedings, informs the standards and duties which arbitrators have to comply with.

If you look at the case law concerning awards involving allegations of bribery, the issues discussed at the level of judicial control very much mirror those we have been hearing about throughout the day: How were the proceedings organised? Should they have been stayed, for example, to take into account information and evidence from criminal proceedings? Was the parties' right to be heard respected? Were all of the relevant legal rules taken into account?

However, what is crucial in all of these cases are the facts of the case and the assessment regarding the legality of money paid or other advantages granted. Did these advantages constitute a bribe, or were they provided in exchange for legitimate services? This is very much a factual question. With respect to the level of judicial control, it consequently matters to what extent courts at the annulment or enforcement stage are prepared to review the factual findings of the tribunal.

The answer to this question differs from jurisdiction to jurisdiction.

In Switzerland, the position resulting from the case law is clear. The prohibition of bribery forms part of public policy,[1] but the assessment of whether or not there has been bribery is a matter to be decided by the arbitral tribunal. The tribunal's assessment is not reviewed by the Federal Supreme Court in annulment proceedings unless the taking of evidence as such gives rise to challenges pursuant to Article 190 PILA.[2]

To obtain the annulment of an award on public policy grounds, the award has to present a clear contradiction between the assessment of the evidence and the conclusions drawn. Basically, the arbitral tribunal must have found bribery but declined to qualify it as such. In practice, this almost never happens.

The practical consequences of this fairly narrow approach can be seen in a number of recent decisions. Companies that are under investigation for bribery or launch an internal investigation because of certain red flags typically stop payments to consultants and other intermediaries whenever there are concerns about the legality of such third-party relationships. Often, payment stops are put in place to meet the expectations of authorities, such as the DOJ or the Serious Fraud Office in the UK, as companies who self-report compliance failures and hope to obtain a deferred prosecution agreement or similar arrangement are expected to show that they are taking strong remedial action to enhance their compliance systems. This change in conduct can lead to conflicts with consultants and other intermediaries, especially in cases where the underlying contract does not provide a clear basis for stopping payments or terminating relationships.

In Switzerland, what transpires from the case law is that companies in these situations cannot really count on the help of the Federal Supreme Court to avoid payment obligations in situations where the arbitral tribunal has previously come to the conclusion that the consultant's claim is justified. What matters is whether illegality can be established in the arbitration; if this is not the case, then the Federal Supreme Court is not going to reverse that analysis.[3]

What are we to make of this? In some ways, this case law shows the gap which often can exist between the perspective of courts and corporate realities. Companies that have found evidence of compliance breaches in their organisation typically are under immense pressure to stop making any dubious payments, whether or not this may mean that they risk breaching contracts with (former) partners. Especially if companies are under scrutiny from powerful enforcement authorities such as the Department of Justice or the UK's Serious Fraud Office, their main focus is on showing full cooperation and compliance with the expectations of the authorities – even if this

1. This was established in a 1993 landmark decision concerning *national power corporation v. Westinghouse*, Swiss Federal Supreme Court, 2 September 1993 (ATF 119 II 380), at para. 4b.
2. *See* Swiss Federal Supreme Court, 2 September 1993 (ATF 119 II 380); 2 August 2013 (ATF 4A_362/2013); 3 March 2014 (ATF 4A_231/2014); 29 January 2015 (ATF 4A_532/2014); 17 January 2013 (ATF 4A_538/2012); 3 November 2016 (ATF 4A_136/2016); 11 July 2017 (4A_50/2017) and, generally, Swiss Federal Supreme Court, 2 September 1993 (ATF 119 II 380), at para. 3c; Swiss Federal Supreme Court, 17 January 2013 (ATF 4A_538/2012), at para. 6.1; Swiss Federal Supreme Court, 26 June 2015 (ATF 4A_231/2014), at para. 5.1.
3. Cf. Swiss Federal Supreme Court, 23 September 2014 (ATF 4A_231/2014); Swiss Federal Supreme Court, 3 November 2016 (ATF 4A_136/2016).

may mean that there may, from a purely contractual point of view, not be a sufficient cause for stopping payments or terminating agreements with individual partners.

In this situation, the Swiss Federal Supreme Court's restrictive approach to the review of arbitral awards means that the responsibility for deciding on the legitimacy of claims raised in response to such measures lies with the arbitral tribunal, whose analysis of the facts and law will not be reviewed in setting-aside proceedings. However, it also is important to realise that this approach is absolutely in line with the court's general and firmly established case law regarding the very limited judicial review in setting-aside proceedings. The recent case law on disputes involving allegations of bribery or compliance breaches, in other words, reflects the general attitude of Swiss arbitration law, where a lot of deference is given to the tribunal, and court oversight is essentially limited to fundamental procedural guarantees.

There is, however, one exception to this principle, and it can be quite relevant in the context of bribery and corruption. This is the possibility to have proceedings reopened by means of revision if new relevant evidence is discovered after the termination of the arbitration or if there are indications that the arbitration was influenced by criminal conduct.[4]

This step was taken in two cases involving allegations of bribery, including in a case which was already mentioned earlier today and which concerned the controversial sale of military vessels from France to Taiwan.[5] In this case, lobbyists had been retained to assist with obtaining regulatory approvals and political support for this controversial transaction. One such intermediary successfully brought a claim in arbitration, arguing that he had not been paid the agreed commission. Twelve years later, the case was reopened after a criminal investigation in France had found evidence that the witness evidence in the arbitration had been manipulated.

The revision procedure allows introducing this type of evidence to obtain the modification or annulment of an award that has already entered into legal force and thus to retroactively correct the factual basis underlying the award. This possibility to introduce new facts and evidence into the arbitration constitutes an important exception to the judicial restraint generally exercised by the Swiss Federal Supreme Court and allows to reopen cases that were concluded before the completion of criminal investigations into allegations of bribery and corruption.

In England, the position is quite similar in the sense that the courts retain the possibility to review evidence in exceptional circumstances and to review fresh evidence but exercise these powers with restraint.

Thus, in a 2016 case concerning a long-term gas supply contract governed by Iranian law, the English High Court refused to overturn an award by a tribunal, which had rejected a defence based on allegations of bribery.[6] As the respondent had not argued the voidability of the contract before the arbitral tribunal, the court was not

4. Swiss Federal Supreme Court, 11 March 1992 (ATF 118 II 199); Swiss Federal Supreme Court, 14 March 2008 (ATF 134 III 286) at para. at 2.1.
5. Swiss Federal Supreme Court, 6 October 2009 (ATF 4A_596/2008); cf. also Swiss Federal Supreme Court, 29 August 2006 (ATF 4P.102/2006).
6. Cf. *National Iranian Oil Company (NIOC) v. Crescent Petroleum Company International Ltd*, [2016] EWHC 510 (Comm.).

prepared to conduct a fresh review of the merits of the case. The judge considered that the factual assessment made by the arbitral tribunal could only be reopened in 'very exceptional circumstances' or in the presence of fresh evidence, which was not found to exist in this case. In enforcement proceedings, the general objective is to privilege the finality of awards. However, it is accepted that the state is not to enforce foreign awards tainted by bribery in situations where this would result in a violation of domestic public policy. In comparison with earlier cases,[7] there is a greater willingness to exceptionally take into account fresh evidence stemming from criminal investigation to reconsider a tribunal's factual assessments at the enforcement stage.[8]

Finally, in France, the situation has in recent years taken a somewhat different turn from what is the case in Switzerland and England. For many years, the Paris Court of Appeal had followed what was known as a 'minimalist approach' by only accepting public policy challenges if the alleged violation was 'blatant, actual and concrete' ('violation flagrante, effective et concrète'). This approach has not remained without criticism and has since been substantially reshaped with respect to cases involving allegations of corruption.[9] Of particular relevance in this regard is an investor-state case, *Republic of Kyrgyzstan v. Belokon*, in which allegations of money laundering had been raised before the tribunal but had not been considered relevant for the outcome of the case. In its annulment application, the state submitted new evidence showing that the investor had entertained close relations with the son of the former president, offshore entities had been used for the transfer of funds without economic necessity, and the investor had in an unrelated matter been convicted of money laundering. In the eyes of the Paris Court of Appeal, these elements constituted 'serious, specific and concurring indicia' of criminal conduct, based on which it annulled the award on public policy grounds. In explaining its decision, the Paris Court of Appeal indicated that it would exercise a comprehensive review of the facts of the case to prevent the recognition or enforcement of awards in situations where the underlying agreement may be illegal as a result of corruption, money laundering or fraud, including where allegations of criminal conduct were considered but rejected as unproven or irrelevant by the arbitral tribunal.[10]

7. The traditional approach is illustrated by a case in which suspicions of bribery had arisen in connection with the supply of military equipment from former Yugoslavia to Kuwait. A related dispute with an intermediary, Westacre, was referred to arbitration in Switzerland. Suspicions of bribery were mentioned, but not pleaded or proven during the arbitration. The resulting award in favour of the intermediary was upheld by the Swiss Federal Supreme Court and ultimately also enforced in England, although additional witness evidence supporting allegations of bribery was made available after the termination of the arbitration, cf. *Westacre Investments Inc. v. Yugoimport SDRP Holding Company Ltd* (1999) QB 740.
8. *BRG Trading (UK) Limited v. Sinocore International Co Limited* [2018] EWCA Civ 838. In a more recent case, the Commercial Court held that it was appropriate to consider fresh expert evidence relating to potential criminal law risks in connection with the execution of an award ordering the defendants to pay a consultant, *see Alexander Brothers Limited v. Alstom Transport SA & Alstom Network UK Limited* [2020] EWHC 814 (Comm).
9. *See also* A-M. Lacoste, *Corruption as Bar to Award Enforcement in France*, (2018), 36, 31 ASA Bulletin.
10. Paris Court of Appeal, Ch. 1, 21 February 2017, No. 15/01650, *Republic of Kyrgyzstan v. V. Belokon*.

This approach has subsequently also been applied in enforcement proceedings and was relied upon to deny enforcement of a Swiss award, which had previously been upheld by the Swiss Federal Supreme Court.[11] The Paris Court of Appeal, in fact, considered that the parties had not had the opportunity to explain whether the agreement underlying the dispute violates international public policy, as understood in France and therefore ordered the parties to produce additional evidence before deciding on the enforcement application. In another case, an English award was denied enforcement on similar grounds.[12]

While each of these cases was rendered against the background of specific facts, the decisions of the Paris Court of Appeal suggest that defences based on allegations of bribery can in France, in principle, be raised for the first time in annulment or enforcement proceedings. Due to this possibility, the judicial control of arbitral awards in cases involving allegations of criminal conduct today tends to go further in France than in England and Switzerland, where no similarly broad review of the tribunal's findings is allowed and where new evidence is only exceptionally taken into account at the annulment or enforcement stage.

Is the French approach better suited to tackling the challenges of bribery and corruption in the context of arbitration? There is no easy answer to this. Arbitral tribunals faced with defences based on allegations of bribery have to navigate murky waters. Blameworthy conduct often exists on more than one side, and arbitral tribunals typically only see a small fraction of a complex set of facts and relationships between multiple actors. It is possible that they are not told the full truth because none of the parties or witnesses is keen on addressing their potential involvement in improper conduct. Arbitral proceedings over contractual claims potentially affected by bribery or corruption often take place long before criminal investigations have come to a conclusion.[13] In many of the complex cross-border cases, criminal proceedings never reach the stage of an indictment, let alone of a conviction, as they are settled beforehand, and it is rare that full light is made on the responsibilities of all the individuals and companies involved.

As a result, there clearly is a possibility that arbitral tribunals may render an award that does not do full justice to all elements of the case. In hindsight, and in consideration of facts that may only emerge gradually through proceedings in different jurisdictions, arbitral awards rendered with respect to a particular claim may well

11. *See* Paris Court of Appeal, Ch. 1, 10 April 2018, No. 16/11182, *Société Alstom Transport SA et al. v. C D Ltd.*, and, for the preceding decision of the Swiss decision rejecting the annulment application, Swiss Federal Supreme Court, 3 November 2016 (ATF 4A_136/2016).
12. Cour de Cassation, 13 September 2017, *Indagro v. Ancienne Maison Marcel Bauche, Rev. Arb.*, 2017/3, 900.
13. Cf., for example, the various proceedings related to investments by the Italian energy company, ENI, and its former subsidiary, Saipem, in connection with the construction of an oil & gas production unit in Algeria. In arbitration proceedings dealing with contractual aspects of this matter, the Algerian-state-owned oil company, Sonatrach, has raised corruption arguments requesting the recovery of more than EUR 160 million in commissions which Saipem allegedly paid through a Hong Kong entity to procure contract. While a settlement was reached in 2018 of these aspects of the case, criminal charges against a number of individuals are currently still pending in Milan, cf. Global Arbitration Review, 28 March 2018, <https://globalarbitrationreview.com/article/1167326/saipem-settles-with-sonatrach-in-shadow-of-bribery-trial>.

appear to be questionable or even incorrect. However, it does not automatically follow from this that national courts are necessarily in a better position to rule on the legitimacy of claims in setting aside or enforcement proceedings and that they should substitute their assessment to that of the tribunal which heard the entire case and formed its view based on the evidence available to it at the time of the proceedings.

This said, arbitrators definitely should look behind the façade of structures and transactions set up to appear legitimate and address potential red flags relevant to the outcome of the case submitted to them. Also, where relevant evidence of bribery or other illegal conduct only becomes available after the termination of the arbitration, it must subject to appropriate procedural safeguards, be possible to take this evidence into account. This helps to strengthen arbitration as a process and ensure that economic actors and society as a whole continue placing trust in arbitration as a process. By contrast, I am not sure that a general broadening of the level of judicial review over the factual assessments made by tribunals is the right approach in this regard. Typically, the courts exercising this review will be more remote from the case than the arbitral tribunal. A systematic review of the tribunal's assessment also will raise difficult delimitation issues, and it might encourage strategic conduct by parties which may actually make it harder for tribunals to tackle bribery and other illegal conduct in the course of the proceedings. Thank you.

**RIKARD WIKSTRÖM-HERMANSEN:**

I have several interesting follow-up questions. We still have a few more minutes, and I want to open the floor.

**PHILIPPE PINSOLLE:**

Just to comment on what you said about French law, there is a bit of confusion here because *Belokon* (check) is a case about treaty law, so a case about jurisdiction.

It is consent that was tested, and I do not believe that the test is different in France and in this country. Both review courts have no limitation when they deal with jurisdiction, so this is not new. It is just a question of assessing whether there was consent because it was a treaty-based case.

What is new is that when it concerns international public policy, which is extremely narrow, it could be corruption, money laundering, that sort of thing, because the court was very careful to say it stressed on the international conventions, then the court said, 'I will review it more carefully'. That is new, but Belokon is not new. Belokon is just a jurisdictional issue.

You have to be very careful when describing the case law.

**ABDULHAY SAYED:**

I want to test a proposition that speaks to two questions raised by Professor Mayer that are related to the attitude of the arbitrator facing suspicions of corruption, and the second which is the standard of proof that ought to be applied whether it is loose or stringent.

I am wondering whether one is able to make a linkage in the decision making with the corruption perception index that we have seen in the first panel. Essentially, one would say that it all depends on the country and the ranking of the country on this corruption perception index. The idea would be the lower the country is on the corruption perception index, the looser the standard of proof ought to be, and the arbitrator should be more prone to becoming intrusive in the proceedings.

**PIERRE MAYER:**

I am not sure why if the standard is low, the duty of the arbitrator would be higher.

**ABDULHAY SAYED:**

I am not linking both. I am suggesting that it may be a presumption that if you are facing a country that is low in ranking in the corruption perception index, it would be more prone to be intrusive and more prone to say the standard of proof ought to be lesser not a stringent one.

**KATE DAVIES:**

I am not sure I agree with that approach. I think the burden of proof and the type of proof that is required to evidence corruption should always be the same regardless of what country you are dealing with. As Professor Mayer rightly said earlier, just because someone comes in and says corruption is endemic in my country does not mean the arbitrator is under a duty to investigate.

What I do think needs to change within the arbitral context is the way in which evidence is evaluated and the type of evidence that is taken into account. If you have a case in which a third-party intermediary is used, and that third-party intermediary engages all of the red flags which are listed in the FCPA's guidelines for corruption, and you then have payments by that agent, all of which are lacking in any kind of receipt or invoice, per the example I gave earlier, in a white-collar context, an investigation context, all of that would be more than sufficient for a finding of corruption. Red flags are used as evidence of corruption because it is so difficult to prove, et cetera.

I think that is what needs to change, not the lowering of the standard of proof. The standard of proof is the standard of proof. I think what you need to look at is the type of evidence that is required or which is sufficient to establish a finding of corruption. That is my own personal view.

**RIKARD WIKSTRÖM-HERMANSEN:**

I tend to agree. Your proposal, which is interesting, but the problem, as discussed by Professor Mayer, is that it is more an issue if you can find tangible – it should never be allowed to just have a wide allegation based on which country you are in, et cetera, to trigger investigations. As Kate said, it is very important that we keep the same evidence thresholds.

**NICOLAS ULMER:**

On the issue of how proactive the arbitrator should be, this discussion, particularly Professor Mayer's, brought back some memories. I will try to be very precise. Three arbitrations, one as a sole arbitrator and I was a young man, a long time ago, the respondent did not appear in this arbitration, a somewhat suspicious consulting contract, but did send a few letters in their native language, but I could read that, saying 'Beware, this a funny contract; this is a funny guy'. That is it. I basically wrote they have not brought any proof; I do not have anything to go with.

In another case, a sports case, one party kept making much more subtle allusions – there is something funny, nothing specific. They made it two or three times but very vague. There was no appetite by the tribunal to look into it, and we did not ask the questions.

I sort of have developed a kind of theory, which I have used with clients; if you are going to raise an issue of public policy and illegality, particularly in something you participated in, you should also – and this is a matter of policy – come forward and be honest and direct about it. You should not try and make use of public policy to queer the proceeding a little bit when you are not prepared to say what it is you are really talking about.

Why? To put it crudely, you should not cover yourself and try to say there is something funny here. That was the approach I took, and I would be interested to know your reactions.

The third case, just to raise something different, was a long-term lease on a holiday resort. As things got nastier in the case, the respondent started to point out more and more that the claimant, who was the lessor, was using an offshore company and was probably doing this not to pay taxes in her home jurisdiction, which was a European country pretty notorious for tax equation. Again, the tribunal had little appetite for this.

Here, there are two things that are different. It did not directly impact the contract between these two parties. It was more what a party was doing with the money, declaring or not afterwards. I think there is another point, which is a bigger one, which is taxation. I have found – and I suspect people in this room would agree – there is a lot more tolerance by people in this room where it is tax evasion as opposed to bribery. It shocks us less.

I would be curious if there are any reactions from the panel or the floor.

**ANNE-CATHERINE HAHN:**

I would support what you said. I think that goes back to what we were discussing before. There is a requirement of specific evidence or indicia, and they must be relevant for the outcome of the case pending in arbitration.

Issues outside of the context of the proceedings may be relevant, but perhaps they are also just invoked to discredit a counterparty. As you suggested, there is a policing power of the arbitral tribunal to make sure that, issues that are relevant but have not been clearly pleaded, are brought to the front in such a way that they can be assessed by a tribunal, rather than remaining a mere insinuation suggesting that the other parties are lacking legitimacy and generally engage in criminal conduct.

Related to this is also the timing of when allegations are brought up. Of course, tactical thinking can influence when allegations of bribery are introduced into proceedings, or maybe only raised after their completion when other defences have failed. I think if we discuss a duty or the power of arbitral tribunals to deal with these things, it also involves the power to control compliance with procedural requirements and to make sure that parties and counsel act transparently.

**PIERRE MAYER:**

I agree. Making reference to your second example, that the simple allegation by a party that there has been corruption is not enough; it does not trigger anything. You may have the feeling that that party just wants to derail the proceedings, so that should not be encouraged.

There must be something specific, not even a vague consideration that gives some credibility. For instance, how do you explain that this intermediary got 10% fees on the main contract? 10% is enormous. He says nothing more. I think if I am the arbitrator, I would like the parties to be more specific on what this intermediary did in practice. I think that is the normal reaction.

I gave the example of the *Metal-Tech* award by a tribunal chaired by Gabrielle Kaufmann-Kohler. For me, that is an excellent attitude. There was something really suspicious.

She wants to go further because suspicion is not enough.

That brings me to a third point, the standard of proof. It has been mentioned, but the normal standard of proof in common law countries is more likely than not the balance of probabilities. In civil law countries, not much attention is brought to the standard of proof.

You can read treaties on civil law under the chapter on Proof; you see nothing under the standard of proof. My impression is that judges in civil law countries, and in France, that is certain, they say – it is my intimate conviction.

What is my intimate conviction? That is more than more likely than not. The standard is much higher, and I do not think it should be changed because it is corruption. It is often said, that has already been mentioned, it is not because corruption is very vexing for the party which is accused of having corrupted that the threshold should be higher because you also have to look at the consequences of corruption and that might even convince you that the threshold should be lower than higher.

**RIKARD WIKSTRÖM-HERMANSEN:**

There we have to conclude. I have enjoyed this discussion. Thank you.

# Panel 4: Role of International Arbitration in Fighting Corruption

*Moderated by Ulrike Gantenberg*

**CHRISTIAN OETIKER:**

Welcome back to the last session. Our final panel today deals with the role of international arbitration in fighting corruption. I am sure that the lively debate so far will continue on this topic. We are happy to have Ulrike Gantenberg here as moderator. She is a partner of Heuking Kühn Lüer Wojtek in Düsseldorf. She holds a degree from the University of Saarland.

As many of our German colleagues do, Ulrike combines the areas of dispute resolution, corporate M&A. In the dispute resolution area, she has a focus on post-M&A, corporate/licence, construction and investor-state disputes.

We are particularly happy to have Ulrike here, as yesterday evening she got stuck in Düsseldorf. I do not know whether she walked here or how she managed to get here, but we are very happy to have her here.

**ULRIKE GANTENBERG:**

Thank you to the organisers for setting up this last panel. We have a difficult task in various ways: one, we are partially truncated, although it does not look like it; the other one is that we are the last panel, and half of the people are gone, and the rest are partially sleeping! Our task is to wake you up and to bring the issue of corruption into life. We will try to pin down some tasks, obligations, risks - and maybe look into the future in order to make sure that arbitration is not the new hub for corrupt people because we close our ears and addict to party autonomy.

We are very happy to have with us Professor Mark Pieth. You know him from the morning session. Professor Pieth steps in, and we are grateful for that because Yves Bertossa suddenly turned ill. We are not the masters of penal law, in particular not on Swiss penal law, so we are very happy to get insight into that.

A short introduction for those who missed the morning session. Professor Mark Pieth is a Professor of Criminal Law in Basel and has served twice as Dean of Basel Law School. He has an Honorary Doctorate from the University of Sussex.

He is a member of various commissions investigating regarding in particular bribery and other crimes, and is always linked and very open to arbitration, including his tool kit for arbitrators, which he set up and discussed earlier in January in Basel. Professor Pieth is the incarnation of the link between penal law and arbitration, so thank you for sharing your insight with us.

Professor Pieth will leave a bit earlier, so that is why we adapted the schedule. After Professor Pieth, we have Koh Swee Yen speaking.

She is a partner with Wong Partnership qualified in Singapore. She practises as counsel and as an arbitrator with a particular focus on commercial law, also investment law, looking much into energy and international sales. She has first-class honours from the National University of Singapore, a particularly talented student with the Singapore Academy of Law prize for being a top student.

We are very lucky you made it here to share your insight into the duty or right of arbitrators to report on suspicion in relation to the other obligations of arbitrators, and that might clash somewhere.

We have with us speaking as the last speaker, Stephan Wilske. He is a partner with Gleiss Lutz in Stuttgart. He has studied in Tübingen, Aix-en-Provence and Chicago and is admitted to the bar in Germany and to various US courts. He is a lecturer at Heidelberg University, Jena and visiting professor at the National Taiwan University.

As you probably will find out later, he has a reputation of being the provocative voice of the German arbitration community, so that is particularly helpful on this topic to wake us all up. The matter deserves critical reflection.

We heard earlier said, that there is this party autonomy and if parties do not answer any more questions; maybe we, as arbitrators, should give up investigating. That is the insight of Panel 3.

We will see if this approach works with penal law. Maybe there are some obligations on the arbitrator itself - in order not to commit a crime - to liaise with public authorities. This is all the more delicate in international arbitration because who is competent if you have three arbitrators coming from different countries, two parties of two further different countries, and they all meet, for example, here in Geneva. So why on earth should Swiss penal law be applicable? That is hopefully where we get some insight.

# Duty to Report Suspicion? Risk for Personal Liability (Aiding and Abetting)?

*Mark Pieth*

**MARK PIETH:**

Thank you very much. I must apologise that I am yet again up here. The challenge is not so easy because stepping into the big shoes of the famous prosecutor, Yves Bertossa, is not going to be easy.

What we are doing is we are talking about the intersection between arbitration and domestic law and specifically law enforcement. The first question that poses itself is: do arbitrators, if they stumble over something that looks very fishy, have an obligation to notify the authorities? I think that is a question that immediately follows the question that you had just discussed before where you were asking yourself: do we, as arbitrators, have a duty to investigate if something does not look very correct?

There you obviously had various situations. You had a situation if a party raised a defence or an argument of corruption, or you had this strange silence that nobody wanted to touch the issue and yet it was in the room. Here now, it is a step further, and we must assume there is a minimum of investigation with the means of the arbitrator and still believe it is fishy, but you might not be able to say it is corruption. The question is: what do I need to do as an arbitrator?

The first question I would put there is: who is going to tell me what to do? This is not a matter of arbitral law. I take that it is primarily a matter of some kind of national law, but which national law. The obvious national law would be the seat. You say: is there regulation at the seat?

There might also be an extension because arbitrators might be subject to their own law that they carry with them around the national principle. We will come back to that in a moment. The seat would be the obvious entry point, I guess.

I started off probably thinking Yves Bertossa would start from Swiss law. There is the first point there. Arbitrators may seem to be somewhere floating between the public and the private domain. They are maybe not judges in the true sense, but they are not entirely private either because what they are producing are awards that will then hopefully be enforceable. There is also an interesting aspect in Swiss law. For instance, an arbitrator that is being bribed is considered a public official, so it is the bribery of a public official if one bribes an arbitrator according to Swiss law. It goes far in the direction of saying arbitrators are actually public officials, yet that does not solve our issue because, in Swiss law, not all officials are obliged to notify offences.

There is a very narrow concept in the Swiss Procedural Code focusing primarily on prosecutors. Basically, the actual prosecutors they have to notify, but the point where I think most everybody comes out is to say, arbitrators, according to Swiss law, would not have an obligation to notify.

Again, it does not solve all questions because it raises the next one. It asks: do you have a right to notify them? That issue will come up when I am asking myself I might be committing an offence myself as an arbitrator doing my work and, therefore, I might want to notify to free myself.

Obviously, there is an issue which is an arbitral issue which I will not touch on; my colleague will do that. The question if I do notify, am I in breach of my private contract with parties, the confidentiality arrangement, and would I be civilly liable for having told on them? That is a different matter. The question is: can I actually notify?

Frankly, if the alternative is to commit a crime, as a criminal lawyer, you would say you are in a conflict of duties, and there we are relatively easy and telling people you do not have to commit a crime, you can liberate yourself.

That is the criminal perspective.

My hunch is that probably a Swiss lawyer would say in civil law it cannot be so much different because if you have that conflict, you have to be able to liberate yourself.

I would argue if there is no obligation, you do have a right, but all this is contingent on Swiss law of the seat being applicable, which is an open issue if that is the correct approach.

Just a word on committing an offence as an arbitrator that is maybe a touchy point.

There are various options possible. One is that by actually forcing a party to make a payment, I would actually help fulfil a bribe promise. The promise itself is an offence, but actually fulfilling the offence is just another part of the offence, and so I might be involved in aiding and abetting.

Similarly, I might become part of a chain of money laundering. That is a very real risk. I can tell you one case that I stumbled over. It was one of my first cases. The case has a name to those who know it, but the official name is the Zurich Ad Hoc Partial Award of 19 October 2004. I leave it at that. The story is interesting. I can anonymise it so much it brings across what the problem was.

In this case, a criminal minister of a country I will not name had given his own shell corporations licenses, and he was trying then, and he had the right, to buy a very big real company, an existing company. He had the right to acquire those shares. Now he came and had all the money and said 'I will acquire this company', USD 4 billion. The other party did not want to hand over the shares and said, 'But your money is extra commercial. We cannot take it; it is dirty money. From A to Z, it is money from crime, so we would become launderers if we took it.'

The problem was it went even further.

In my expert opinion, I wrote it is questionable whether the tribunal can take any money from this party because whatever they take, they will be then in a situation of being launderers. If it is an ad hoc context, we do not have an intermediate body to pre-launder; they would have taken the money themselves. They were at a real risk of laundering.

They apparently continued with their work. They did not stop proceedings. They said, yes, this is a case of money laundering. It led to four arbitrations tipping one after the other in favour of money laundering. It was one of the first really big cases. The fear obviously was that one would become involved in laundering money.

You, of course, are familiar with other similar situations where people in maybe a less complicated way simply use the tribunal to generate a title where they are not really fighting, where the parties are just agreed that one party will lose the case and then say we have to pay because of this arbitral award.

To sum up, a tribunal is not obliged to notify, in my view, certainly if Swiss law is applicable, but it has the right certainly when it comes anywhere close to committing a criminal offence itself.

You had asked me to raise one practical question. What happens if Mr Bertossa does get such notification? What will he do? Will he put it in the waste paper basket? Possibly, yes.

Why? Is he then the right person to receive it? He will look at it through the lens of jurisdiction: where is the place of the offence? Then, of course, the whole story starts from the beginning again.

If somebody is trying to cheat the court in order to generate an interesting outcome from them, then there is a territorial nexus. If money laundering is being committed here, there is a territorial nexus, but there might be situations where actually there is no real jurisdictional nexus to Switzerland or to Geneva. Then he would probably not touch the issue at all. He would say, 'Sorry, it is not my business.'

I think you asked would he hand it over to somebody else. Maybe, maybe not. He is not obliged. I will leave it at that.

**ULRIKE GANTENBERG:**

We have two or three questions to be clear as to where we stand. One thing is, as long as the place of arbitration is Geneva, we could go to Mr Bertossa if there is money laundering on the way, and Mr Bertossa would initiate whatever investigations if there is no other person with Swiss nationality.

**MARK PIETH:**

The difficulty is he has a different perspective. His perspective is: am I competent here in Geneva for what is being done and that might digress if no crime is being committed or has been committed in Geneva if it just happens to be the seat here and it is kind of convenient for the arbitrators to go to Mr Bertossa and he will tell you 'Thank you very much, but it is the wrong place.'

**ULRIKE GANTENBERG:**

Taking your example of money laundering, I see the point that the money is probably dirty money by which arbitrators would be paid and institutions. What is the choice of the arbitrators? They see there is money laundering on the way. If they go to Mr Bertossa because of whatever relation and they disclose they are working on a money laundering case, in any event, if they disclose, are they still not entitled to take the money? Would they work for free and dismiss the claim on jurisdiction on the merits? Is that the life of an arbitrator in a money laundering case?

**MARK PIETH:**

Your question has two dimensions: one is a criminal law dimension. People ask – has anything actually happened yet, or are we in a pre-phase where somebody is preparing? Have they tried to launder, or have they started?

By asking the tribunal or court to make a decision, we might be advancing towards an attempt. He will ask himself as a criminal lawyer: are we anywhere close to crime yet? That is one set of issues.

**MICHAEL SCHNEIDER:**

Counsel has the problem.

**ULRIKE GANTENBERG:**

The question again is – why is Mr Bertossa competent if the counsel comes from Sweden?

**MICHAEL SCHNEIDER:**

Executing in Geneva.

**MARK PIETH:**

We have the underlying offence, and that might have been committed already. Then we move into the money laundering dimension, and there maybe they have not even started yet. It just sticks, and the question is what they are requesting the tribunal to do, whether that really falls under a criminal attempt. Those are issues that he will ask himself.

The other question was what more happens?

**ULRIKE GANTENBERG:**

How can an arbitrator protect himself? The case is there. The possibility of an arbitrator is to step back, and the next one will come. They will find a blind and deaf person.

**MARK PIETH:**

There we are in an arbitral question again. That is not a criminal law question necessarily. The question is – what do you do? Do you say there is no jurisdiction? That would be a solution, not a very satisfactory solution because you will go unpaid if you cannot touch the money.

**ULRIKE GANTENBERG:**

That is the end of the story: whatever the tribunal does, they cannot touch the money.

**MARK PIETH:**

Yes. That is not very attractive.

**ULRIKE GANTENBERG:**

It does not sound attractive! Before we turn to the point – how can an arbitrator, and should an arbitrator, go to the authorities? We understand there is no obligation, but there could be a right, and if I do not take the money, then maybe I do not have an obligation because I do not need to protect myself. Assuming an arbitrator goes to the public authorities, does that person, with the right moment, what would be the right moment? It could be in a pre-phase so that no authority works, and the entire penal law becomes a toothless tiger because no one is competent, and you are too early. That does not help an arbitrator who is courageous.

If it is the right moment, or even if the arbitrator contacted the authorities, is there an obligation to inform the parties, or is it even worse to inform the parties because the parties could then cover whatever penal actions are on the way? That would conflict on the arbitral side, and that Swee Yen will cover with the obligation of confidentiality and transparency and all the nice things we have set up.

**MARK PIETH:**

You realise it is quite a complicated field. There are different situations. One situation is you have the classic case in the past. There are two parties, and you realise the bribery has already taken place. They are now trying to claim their bribe; the intermediary turns up and says, 'I want my bribe', or do you want to enforce a contract even though it is tainted by bribery? That is the easier case because the risk that you would then become an accomplice *post factum* is not really very big unless there is a risk of money laundering. That is really in the practical situation. If the crime has been committed, it is done so you would look at additional crimes that kick in after the original crime.

There is another aspect which we have not talked about yet. If I was Mr Bertossa, I would troop in and seize all the money that is floating around. You have to imagine everything is seized and then sort it out later on. That is the first step that he would take. He is interested in the money. Again, that does not help arbitration very much.

Your question would be, from an arbitrator's perspective, what is the right moment. I think you had on your original list the overcautious arbitrator. If I come too early and there is nothing substantive around, that will just cause trouble for everybody, and the prosecutor will not move; they will not do anything. If I come too late when I have taken the money that is tainted, that is also not very good, so I have to actually find a way in between those two extremes. There is a possibility to talk to Mr Bertossa and say 'Would you take this? Would you regard yourself as competent?' Again, you have the right but not the obligation. The only reason why you would do it is because you do not want to run into trouble yourselves.

**ULRIKE GANTENBERG:**

Thank you for your insight. We come now to Swee Yen Koh, who will go on the arbitrator's side to see if, and to what extent, there may be other obstacles or duties to report.

# Duty or Right of Arbitrators to Report Suspicion of Corruption to Authorities?

*Koh Swee Yen*

**KOH SWEE YEN:**

Thank you for staying for the last session. First, I want to thank ASA for inviting me here as well.

I am going to focus on the question: is there a duty of an arbitrator to report corruption, to report suspicion of corruption, and how does this duty conflict or how does it sit with an obligation of confidentiality, if, indeed, there is an obligation of confidentiality on arbitrators in international arbitration?

First, Professor Pieth stated that there is actually no obligation on an arbitrator, and not just on an arbitrator, but on any person, to report corruption or suspicion of corruption under Swiss law. For instance, if you are a Swiss tribunal member and you have come across corruption, even very clear cases of corruption, under Swiss law, there is no obligation or duty on you to report.

This position is actually not unique to Switzerland. I have carried out a search and found out that even under the Foreign Corrupt Practices Act ("FCPA") of the United States or under the UK Bribery Act, there is also no general duty to report violations of the anti-bribery law to the authorities. This is also something which you can find in quite a number of other jurisdictions. There may be an obligation to report under US law in circumstances of securities violation and various other acts, but the duty to report corruption, not to mention suspicion of corruption, is actually not found in the anti-bribery laws.

It may be interesting to know that the laws of certain jurisdictions may actually impose a duty to report corruption and suspicion of corruption. For example, in Vietnam and South Africa, such an obligation is imposed on those who are persons of authority. The law to which the tribunals' members are personally subject may give rise to the question of whether you have a duty to report corruption and suspicion of corruption.

Now I would like to share with you the position of Singapore which is quite interesting. Under the bribery law, there is no duty to report corruption per se, but we have what is known as the Corruption, Drug Trafficking and Other Serious Crimes (Confiscation of Benefits) Act ("CDSA"). This is a legislation found in various other jurisdictions too. Pursuant to section 39(1) of the CDSA, where a person knows or has reasonable grounds to suspect that any property represents the proceeds of, or was used in connection with, or is intended to be used in connection with, any act which constitutes criminal conduct, in this instance it covers corruption, and this is a matter which came to his knowledge or suspicion in the course of his true profession, business or employment, then he shall disclose this knowledge or suspicion to what is known as the Suspicious Transaction Reporting Officer as soon as practicably possible.

In a situation where a tribunal member who is subject to Singapore law actually knows that there are certain monies which are proceeds of corruption or proceeds of criminal conduct, even money laundering, they have a duty to report.

What is interesting about this legislation in Singapore is that it is specified in section 39(4) that notwithstanding the general provision in section 39(1), which I have just shared with you, nothing in that provision, and this is specifically provided, makes it an offence for an arbitrator to fail to disclose any information or other matter which came to his attention in the course of any arbitral proceedings in which he acted as an arbitrator. This is very interesting. You have a duty to report if the corruption came to your knowledge in the course of your profession, yet the law says if you are an arbitrator, and you are aware of the corruption in the course of performing your duties, and you fail to disclose it, it will not constitute an offence.

Then, there is another provision under section 39(6) of the CDSA stating, however, that where a person discloses in good faith to an officer, the disclosure shall not be treated as a breach of any restriction upon the disclosure imposed by law, contract or use of professional conduct, and he shall not be liable for any loss arising out of disclosure or act or omission in consequence of this disclosure. An arbitrator who is subject to this particular statute really, I think, knows no better. You are first told you have a duty to report any knowledge of the proceeds of any act which may constitute criminal conduct. You are then, in a sense, protected to say if you do not disclose it, it does not mean that you commit an offence. Then it goes on to say but if you in good faith disclose it, let me tell you that you will also be fine because you will not be found liable in law for any loss arising out of this disclosure.

At the end of the day, I think this legislation puts it down right to the arbitrator himself or herself to decide whether, in that situation, where there is corruption or where there is even suspicion of corruption, bearing in mind reasonable grounds to suspect is sufficient to trigger under this legislation and to make his or her own decision as to 'should I report or not?'.

In fact, in a situation where you have a legislation like this, and the arbitrator decides on reasonable grounds of suspicion to report this to a Suspicious Transaction Reporting Officer, he or she is in a 'nice' position because he or she is protected by the law from not being liable for any loss arising out of this disclosure. A lot of arbitrators are concerned with the possibility of an action for damages for breach of confidence in the event that they do disclose and do report this to the investigative authorities. With that particular legislative provision, an arbitrator is obviously, in a sense, protected and in a much better position.

I will now move on to talk more about the obligation of confidentiality. Another law that may possibly govern the duty of an arbitrator to report corruption or suspicion of corruption is the law of the seat of arbitration. Why do I say the law of the seat of arbitration? It may be that, even though under the penal law, you are not obliged to report corruption, could it be said that under arbitration law and the New York Convention, it is your duty as an arbitrator to produce a valid and enforceable award? Therefore, if you know that this award and the contract or that the final decision is one that is tainted by corruption and may potentially be set aside for being in breach of public policy, would you then say that because of your duty to issue an award that is valid and enforceable, you shall therefore have a duty to report corruption or suspicion of corruption? This is something we can discuss in greater detail.

Next, I want to address the question of why arbitrators may be a bit cautious when it comes to reporting. I think it boils down to this notion that there is this general obligation of confidentiality that applies to all international arbitration.

In fact, the question and the issue of confidentiality in itself, I would say, is a myth because it is not that clear. It is not always the case that all arbitrations are confidential. All arbitrations may be private, meaning that only the parties in the arbitration can be involved, can participate, can attend the hearings, but it does not mean they are confidential in the sense that there is an obligation of confidentiality imposed on parties to the arbitration and the arbitrator not to disclose information that is obtained in the course of arbitration.

Why do I say that? Because if you look at the New York Convention, and you look at other laws, they are silent on the obligation of confidentiality. When you look at the law of the seat of the arbitration, the domestic legislation varies from jurisdiction to jurisdiction. The US Federal Arbitration Act, the Swiss law, the English Arbitration Act, or the Japanese Arbitration Act are all silent on whether there is an obligation of confidentiality in international arbitrations.

In certain jurisdictions, such as Hong Kong or New Zealand, you may have an express provision in the legislation that says there is an obligation of confidentiality, but in all these provisions, they always have these exceptions that say that no party may publish, disclose or communicate any information related to the arbitration proceedings unless they are obliged to by law, which goes back to the first question. In some jurisdictions, they make it quite clear that there is no confidentiality obligation.

The issues of confidentiality obligations and whether an arbitration is confidential, and whether parties are obliged not to disclose information are fundamentally down to the parties' agreement. In certain jurisdictions, they may find that there is an implied obligation of confidentiality, for instance, under English law, Singaporean law, and, I believe, under Swiss law as well.

When it comes to this question of confidentiality, I do not think it is necessarily an answer to not reporting by saying that 'I am not reporting this particular corruption or this suspicion of corruption because I am bound by confidentiality.'

Why do I say that there is a problem? Because the first question you have to answer is: is really there an obligation of confidentiality that is imposed on the parties?

I should draw your attention to institutional rules which, if they are incorporated as part of the arbitration agreement, do impose confidentiality obligations, as I have seen in the SIAC Rules but not necessarily other institutional rules. The first question to answer is always: is there an obligation of confidentiality?

The next question to ask: if there is an obligation of confidentiality, does that mean that I do not have to report, or should I say that this actually falls within an exception to confidentiality because of the question of public interest?

I want to touch briefly on a case that was heard before the Singapore High Court. It is a decision issued in 2011. I found that it was a very interesting case, and we can draw a lot of insights from this case on the factual matrix. What happened in the case was there was a litigation that was commenced. Subsequent to that, the parties applied to stay the litigation in favour of arbitration. They entered into a consent order to refer the matter to arbitration. In that instance, when they referred it to arbitration, there was no express provision of confidentiality, and they also did not adopt the SIAC Rules for the arbitration. A partial award was granted. One of the parties then applied to set aside the award and failed.

Subsequently, in the course of the arbitration, after the partial award was issued, one of the parties decided to go to the Commercial Affairs Department, which is the police division in Singapore and disclosed various documents that he had obtained in the course of discovery in the arbitration. It made various allegations of cheating, tax avoidance, and general criminal conduct.

The other party found out about this and started an action in the Singapore court to set aside the consent order. It started an action to injunct the arbitration for further proceeding on the basis that the former party has repudiated the arbitration agreement by making the police report and by disclosing confidential information to the police, which was in breach of the fundamental condition of the arbitration agreement which was that of confidentiality.

When the courts had to analyse this question, they actually went through a lot of issues. The first question they had to consider was whether there was an implied obligation of confidentiality. The answer was yes. They further addressed the next question: was this implied obligation of confidentiality a condition of the arbitration agreement? The courts said, no, it was not a condition because it was not an express term; thus, it did not deprive the parties substantially of the benefit of the arbitration agreement, and it was not imposed by statute.

The courts then went on to say: 'But, let us look at this obligation of confidentiality. Even if you only look at it and you may say that it is something that is very important, are there exceptions to this obligation of confidentiality?' The courts analysed it and said obviously there are exceptions to this obligation of confidentiality, and one of the key exceptions is that of public interest if the public interest requires disclosure. The courts further asked: whether disclosure of confidential information arising out of arbitration to the relevant authorities where there is reasonable suspicion of criminal conduct would be a breach of confidentiality at all or does it fall as an exception or does it operate as a defence to a breach of confidentiality?

The court went through the authorities and reached the conclusion that when an arbitrator discloses reasonable suspicion of criminal conduct to the authorities, it will amount to an exception to confidentiality. I think this is a very significant decision for two reasons: first, it does admit and recognises that an arbitrator going to the authorities to disclose a reasonable suspicion of criminal conduct is something that is deemed as public interest and would fall as an exception to the confidentiality.

The second takeaway from this is that because it is an exception and not a defence, it means that the arbitrator is not actually in breach of confidentiality obligations. If the arbitrator is in breach of confidentiality obligations, it can potentially subject him or her to damages and claim for damages which we can explore further.

Why did I say this is something that we can draw insights from in this position, as a way forward whether the arbitral community can do more, whether we can do more in the context of corruption and dealing with suspicion of corruption? We have heard earlier today, and I will end with this, the difficulties that arbitral tribunals have when they are confronted with corruption allegations. They are particularly in a difficult position, as Professor Mayer said, where the parties do not plead the corruption allegations, yet the arbitrator still has knowledge that there is something dirty going on, but because it is not pleaded by the parties, the tribunal never gets to decide it. There are also complaints about whether a tribunal is in a position to assess evidence of corruption. This is difficult even for prosecutors and public authorities who have all the powers of subpoena.

Could we mitigate all these difficulties with a more robust approach to reporting corruption, i.e., with arbitral tribunals taking a more robust approach towards reporting corruption to the relevant authorities? This is something I leave with you and which we may want to discuss further.

**ULRIKE GANTENBERG:**

We want to integrate a tiny question and answer session here because Professor Pieth will have to leave early.

For us on the panel, somehow, it appears to me we turn in circles. We say there is an obligation of confidentiality, but there is an exception if an obligation exists by law to disclose. We heard in Swiss law there is no obligation, but I can. Does my little loophole to disclose and to report ever open up? I understand there is a right to protect myself, but that is at the very end. Is it in the end that the tribunal is left on its own with the uncertainty? Does arbitration need to find different solutions because apparently, it is too international?

**KOH SWEE YEN:**

I wanted to follow up on the last point. Perhaps tribunal members should stop looking at the question: should I investigate more into this corruption allegation in this arbitration? Should I be calling up more evidence? If they feel they are in that situation, report to the relevant authorities, the right prosecutor. As you say, if you report to Mr Bertossa and it has nothing to do with Switzerland, he may not take any action.

**MARK PIETH:**

For me, I make a distinction between corruption and money laundering. If I look at corruption, we have heard earlier on that there is this distinction between the problems with the bribed contract, and of course, that is delicate if I am used to enforce the bribe contract. That is when the intermediary comes and calls the tribunal to help him actually obtain his bribe.

The alternative situation that somebody is actually trying to enforce a bribe-tainted underlying contract is really a civil law issue, basically. They had the question, is this underlying contract null and void, or is it just a question that there is something wrong with it that maybe we can solve with damages. Therefore, I do not think the criminal law comes in very quickly. Really your primary interest would be on corruption or the action of enforcement of a bribery contract.

Money laundering again means that there is tainted money. There has to be money that stems from crime, and maybe simplifying and making it applicable on a worldwide basis means that you help transfer those tainted funds outside the reach of the competent law enforcement agency across the border. That would be the point where one has to be careful.

Within that box is, for me also, the situation that I am actually taking tainted money knowingly. I am aware that it is most probably tainted money and then using it for my own purposes. That is where it gets delicate again. It is true that in many cases notifying could be a way out, but I do not think we should fall into a kind of hysteria.

We should see where the points where I am really being used as an accessory are; otherwise, I would do what you are doing and what we have discussed today. Use your means: either deny jurisdiction or deal with the issue on merits.

**CAROLINE MING:**

I would like to share with you one experience some people I know have made, who are not in the room right now but subject to discussion. An arbitrator was suspecting that there was a problem with the transaction, and he was wondering what he was supposed to be used for. He could not get proper answers from either party and at some point, we discussed what he should do. He was feeling very uncomfortable. He certainly did not want to aid any wrongful transaction and be part of it.

Finally, what he did was to ask more and more questions, and at some point, he even told the parties – he reported this to me, so I am not a first-hand speaker – that he had very serious suspicions or problems with the transaction and with the whole process. He told the parties he would not stop questioning, and he would not render any award until he has all answers in his opinion. He basically pushed the parties to settle and/or withdraw the case and for sure not to ask for an award on consent. The parties eventually withdrew. I do not know if they settled, but at least they withdrew the case. It is a tactic.

**ULRIKE GANTENBERG:**

This is probably one of the many difficulties sole arbitrator tribunals are facing. If you ask too much and there is a deal between the parties, they need the award for something else; probably you are left on your own because they settle out of court, or you rescind, or you go and dismiss it. This is probably not much alternative to have unless you have an institution that supports it.

What did the institution do? The sole arbitrator can be particularly lonely in these cases.

**CAROLINE MING:**

The sole arbitrator was particularly lonely, and he made me come back from holidays because I am the institution. We reviewed the case, and we discussed it together, and we came to the conclusion that the best way was to get the parties to withdraw the case, which they did.

**ULRIKE GANTENBERG:**

Which is closing eyes and ears; it is a toothless tiger. That opens up the door for arbitration becoming the hub for corruption and everything because either nobody is competent, you are too quick, too early, in the wrong place. That is a bit delicate.

That neatly brings to Stephan's intervention, who tries to bring up some new ideas and, unfortunately, also obligations and tasks on institutions at least to maybe assist tribunals in order to protect the integrity of arbitration.

# Is There a Need for Further Action and Initiatives by the Arbitration Community?

*Stephan Wilske*

**STEPHAN WILSKE:**

At the risk of being impolite, may I ask a question to the Swiss attendees? If I am a representative of the state of 'Corruptia' and I am looking for the ideal place of arbitration, I see here a competitive advantage for Geneva Switzerland because if this overly curious and interfering arbitrator, who has concerns, is going to the state prosecutor he will be sent away with the comment 'We are not interested in this stuff.'

Now my question as a representative of the state of 'Corruptia': Can I go against this arbitrator for violating his or her confidentiality obligation? Because he/she has to be quiet, he/she has to play the three monkeys [see no evil, hear no evil, speak no evil], and has not complied with that obligation? What do the Swiss attendees think? Can the arbitrators not do anything? On the contrary, they are bound to be silent and play stupid, correct?

I was asked this morning whether I have something to say or whether I have PowerPoint slides. I am fully aware that the copyright for this question is with Wolfgang Peter. I have some PowerPoint slides, and I leave it up to you whether I have something to say.

The organisers requested that I be brief and provocative, and in return, I asked for a place close to the exit, which somehow did not work out, so I will need to be a bit cautious!

I have heard that at yesterday's SCIA Innovation Conference, a US speaker compared the Willem C. Vis Moot Court to arbitration reality and the 45th US President, which was considered to be grossly unfair. To the more sensitive people in this room, here comes a warning: Pursuant to the standards used yesterday against James Boykin, I will be unfair as well. With this warning, let me start.

This is how I will put in my two cents to this discussion. I will describe in a very subjective, maybe even unfair manner the status quo of the discussion on arbitration and corruption. I will ask the question – what can be done *concretely* by arbitral institutions? Yes, by arbitral institutions, not these poor arbitrators who are kind of helpless.

Professor Pieth told us this morning the arbitrators have to re-invent the wheel every time. If they go to the prosecutor, the prosecutor is not interested in that. I am not calling for the prosecutor. I am not responsible for our Geneva prosecutor Yves Bertossa not being here. For me, it is the arbitral institutions that should be in the spotlight. They are getting money for their services. They have a certain brand which they are selling. They should have a close look at what is going on. I offer humble conclusions on timeless wisdom from the wife of a former U.S. president. Consider who that might be?

## The Conceptionalist's and the Dogmatist's Approach

Is there a need for further concrete actions and initiatives by the arbitral community? I see, based on my subjective perception, two approaches: the one I call the approach of the conceptionalist's or the dogmatist's approach, the dream of autonomous arbitration, completely delocalised, not controlled by national laws, and of course there is no need for a Geneva prosecutor.

Until two years ago, I would have called this the French approach. Meanwhile, the French *Cour de Cassation* is meddling so much with arbitration. I would name my old friend Julian Lew for this approach, and I refer you to his brilliant intellectual Freshfields lecture of 2005, published in 'Arbitration International', '*Achieving the Dream: Autonomous Arbitration*'.[1]

There is a special Swiss phenomenon; this is the paranoia of over-regulation. I read with great interest Michael Schneider's contribution – intellectually fascinating, almost satirical – to the Liber Amicorum for Serge Lazareff.[2] The message is: We are wasting our time with regulation; let us go back to the good old times when some very honourable grand seigneur arbitrators were meeting in the Cafe de Paix and investing much time in very sophisticated discussions which are still in the law books today.

I still recall the public outcry by the ASA board two or three years ago when the IBA had issued *Guidelines on Party Representation in International Arbitration*. That was considered to be the end of civilised international arbitration as we know it.[3] The approach of the conceptualists and the dogmatists seems to be: 'Look, this is arbitration. There is no need to do anything. We are completely autonomous. Please get rid of these public prosecutors. The good thing is they do not care about us either.'

---

1. Julien D. M. Lew, *Achieving the Dream: Autonomous Arbitration*, 22(2) Arb. Int'l (2006), 179-204.
2. Michael E. Schneider, *The Essential Guidelines for the preparation of Guidelines, Directives, Notes, Protocols and other methods intended to help international arbitration practitioners to avoid the need for independent thinking and to promote the transformation of errors into 'best practices'*, Liber Amicorum, en l'honneur de Serge Lazareff, 2011, 563-568.
3. Stephan Wilske, *Sanctions Against Counsel in International Arbitration – Possible, Desirable or Conceptual Confusion?*, 8(2) Contemp. Asia Arb. J. (2015), 141, 159-161.

## The Pragmatists' or Business People's Approach

The other approach I would call the approach by the pragmatists or the business people's approach: Do not fix it if it is not completely broken; that is still good until my retirement from the system. The other pragmatic argument for not doing anything is the competitive advantage I just described: Let us not soil our own nest; it only helps our competitors if we do something. That means: Let us deny the existence of the problem, let us marginalise it, only 50% of the procurement contracts from the state of 'Corruptia' are kind of tainted with corruption, the other 50% are good. Come on; this is not so bad;[4] it is only a matter of perspective.

Or let us ridicule everyone who comes up with this topic, which should be a non-topic. Anyway, it is much too dangerous to do something because you do not know exactly what you find if you illuminate the dark corners of international arbitration.

That actually reminds me of some words of wisdom by my favourite English contemporaneous philosopher and guitar player, Keith Richards: '*The cops, I can't involve them, God knows what they could find.*'[5] Let us not talk about this. My fair or unfair observation on the status quo is that there is a certain attitude of 'Do not dig too deep; it might create a bad smell.'

Now, what could be done very concretely by arbitral institutions if they want to get rid of the smell:

## Proclaim the 'Rules of the Game'

The Swiss Chambers could say, 'We have no interest in administering arbitrations which are based on corruption.' They could announce, 'We have a close look at arbitrations when it gets stinky.' ASA could tell its members, 'If you are proved to be involved in corruption-tainted arbitrations, we kick you out of ASA.' The Chartered Institute of Arbitrators is doing things like that if their members misbehave.[6] That would be a clear programme by an institution if they want to take a firm position.

## Mandatory Compliance Programmes for Arbitrators

I have to run every year an online programme on money laundering where I have to answer certain questions. If I fail to give the correct answers, I have to do it again. That is ten minutes. Why should it be below the dignity of an arbitrator prior to being confirmed or appointed as arbitrator to go through an awareness programme on corruption and money laundering?

---

4. Cf. (in the context of the arbitration guerrilla phenomenon) Felix Dasser, *Critical Analysis of the IBA Guidelines on Party Representation* in New Developments in International Commercial Arbitration, 2014, 63, 87 (Christoph Müller et al. (eds), 2014) ('*One could see this as a glass that is half empty or half full*').
5. Keith Richards, *Robbed Blind* from his Album Crosseyed Heart (2015).
6. *See* Stephan Wilske, *International Arbitration and Its Dark Sides, in Particular Corruption: What Arbitral Institutions Could and Should Do to Tackle Such Unwelcome Issues,* 12(2) Contemp. Asia Arb. J. (2019), 147, 164 with a concrete example.

That would not necessarily need the time it took yesterday to describe the ASA arbitration toolbox; that could be shorter. There could be questions to make people aware of red flags. Is it acceptable for a Swiss Rules arbitrator to accept a bonus payment in cash if the arbitrators waive all questions to the parties? I could imagine some people would say if you tax this extra payment, where is the problem?

If an arbitrator candidate has a vanity issue with that by saying, 'I am Mr or Mrs Very Important, I am not running a ten minutes compliance programme', I would ask: 'Do you need Mr or Mrs Very Important anymore?' A mandatory ten-minute compliance programme prior to appointment in order to know a little bit about your arbitrators and advise them of what red flags are does not look like over-regulation to me but rather like a wise and forward-looking policy.

### Corruption Ombudsman or Ombudswomen

What is wrong with a person at the arbitral institution who has the institutional knowledge to assist parties and arbitrators? If you have an issue in an ICC arbitration, who do you contact? The counsel, this twenty-four-year-old Latin American counsel who has no idea? Shall I call Alexis Mourre every time? If there is one person who is in charge of these issues and collects the institutional wisdom, what is wrong with that? It does not cost so much.

Maybe we can even convince Michael Schneider that this is not yet the over-regulation overkill. It would certainly be a job programme for Mark Pieth's disciples. It could be done part-time. It is just like the data protection officer, et cetera. At some point, somebody gets the title but, at least there is someone to contact if an arbitrator has a concern and wants to talk with someone knowledgeable at the institution.

### Blacklist Counsel and Parties Who Were Proved to Be Associated with Corruption in Arbitration

Yes, you lose the business of these people, but again do you really want the business and company of these black sheep for your institution? Arbitral institutions should know that a bad reputation ('the number 1 arbitral institution for money-laundering, murky business disputes and people you don't want to meet outside the hearing room') might easily translate into bad business. Insofar, a 'no question asked' approach might not be a promising long-term business strategy.

### Call for Transparency in 'Corruption in Arbitration'

We heard Thomas Werlen this morning. He was presenting the top ten offenders of the Foreign Corrupt Practices Act. Why does ASA not put parties, counsel, arbitrators on the home page who were proved to be associated with corruption? It may be that this might help. It might deter serious parties. Some counsel would even tell you, 'That is good for me because I am specialised in black sheep, so they know how to find me.' I understand transparency is very fashionable; why not have some transparency here in this case?

### Do Not Accept the Usual Excuses for Inaction

Please do not wait for international solutions. And, certainly, this is not a call for a 'Global Corruption in Arbitration Council'.[7] I perfectly understand that whenever people feel something should be done, but in reality, they do not want anything to be done, there are always three tools available: (1) we need to do much more research, we need a lot of statistical data etc.; (2) we need to wait for an international solution and as long as the arbitral institution of Papua New Guinea is not interested in that, we are not doing anything; (3) let us have an 'international committee' or a galactic or, at least, global council. That sounds like real action but takes two years to argue on the basic principles, it takes another year to discuss diversity, who will sit on the board, and another half a year later, the project is completely forgotten because there is no more funding. This is not what I am calling for.

### Conclusion

My very humble conclusion: Further concrete action has to be done by arbitral institutions. If you do not do anything, if you simply duck away, at some point, real regulation will come, real tough state regulation. Thus, do not hide behind dogmatism and buzz words like confidentiality, party autonomy, and over-regulation; these are all excuses.

Almost everything can be done by arbitral institutions.

My final word of wisdom: if you are offered fishy business, simply follow the advice of the wife of the 40th President of the United States and just say 'No!'

Thank you for your attention.

**ULRIKE GANTENBERG:**

It sounds like we shift from the arbitrators to the institution, the responsibility and tasks, and what do we do with ad hoc arbitration. We are stuck on the arbitrator again.

I open the floor to invite you to discuss how to deal with it, how to handle things, how to work inside the tribunal? If one person thinks there is a fishy issue and the others are closing eyes and ears, who calls the ombudsman or is it simply a non-solution topic where individual courage must live?

**WOLFGANG HAHNKAMPER:**

First, something that came to my mind in between and it is that I do not think that it is the duty of the institution to help the arbitrator out. It should assist, but it is finally his or her own decision to solve the situation, and we have been around that all the time.

Second, I love to carry out my job as an arbitrator when I am appointed, but if I should get into situations where I get all that condensed headache that we were hearing before and discussing before, why do I not simply go back to the legal rooms for

7. *See* Stephan Wilske, *Sanctions Against Counsel in International Arbitration – Possible, Desirable or Conceptual Confusion?*, 8(2) Contemp. Asia Arb. J. (2015), 141, 164-166, with a summary of the idea of the envisaged 'Global Arbitration Ethics Council', suggested by ASA Board members.

contract on works where I find that my product that I have to deliver is – I know it is not undisputed – an enforceable award. If all these circumstances or a sum of them arise, I really have doubts that what comes out would be an enforceable award, which means that the performance is impossible. That would enable and give me the right to withdraw without any consequences. I would do that at that point.

**NIKOLAUS PITKOWITZ:**

I want to respond to Stephan Wilske because I also have an institutional role. I also have the hat of the Vice-President of the Vienna International Arbitral Centre. I say that I think those are issues which are really serious for any institution, and at the VIAC, we established half a year ago a working group on compliance, which I have the honour of heading, and we have developed a number of rules and systems. One is a leaflet for all the arbitrators with special information about their obligations and duties, also an opportunity to get information, also announcement, which is still not yet there but on the website, for the parties to be aware that certain information, particularly when it comes to sanctions and money laundering, cannot be and must not be treated confidential and some other means.

What we had not had at this stage we have not invited Stephan Wilske to become a member of the working group, but that may be a good opportunity now.

I think there is an obligation of institutions, and at IFCA, there is a general organisation of arbitration institutions, and the VIAC has brought this up as a topic so that the arbitration institutions will take a consolidated approach. I think it is in the interests of all arbitration institutions to have a solid, open and transparent approach here.

**STEPHAN WILSKE:**

I did not know of this initiative before but this is exactly what I am asking for, that the institutions take some responsibility and do not shift everything to the arbitrators and close their eyes and ears and leave you with the twenty-four-year-old assistant counsel on the telephone who should tell you what to do.

**ULRIKE GANTENBERG:**

We have exhausted and left you alone with that issue. Thank you very much to everybody for listening to this late and being confident that maybe one day we hopefully find a solution for all that.

Thank you to the organisers for having given the floor and the opportunity to participate.

**BERNHARD BERGER:**

Dear remaining participants, dear members and friends of ASA, some of you might be surprised to see a Vice-President delivering the closing remarks but rest assured there is nothing dirty going on here, no corruption, no bribes involved! I simply have the pleasure to replace our President, Elliott Geisinger, who could unfortunately not make it due to a hearing in Miami. He is extending and sending you all his best regards.

That said, I hope you had the same pleasure as I had, spending a thrilling day here in Geneva on corruption and arbitration. If I look at the programme, the purpose of the conference had been described there 'to explore how the arbitration community should deal with challenges associated with corruption in arbitration.' I have to admit that I am quite satisfied to note that the endemic term 'best practice' has not popped up throughout the day.

As we have seen, there are no clear answers, and many of the issues remain controversial. That does not mean, in my view, that this conference did not live up to its objective. On the contrary, I would submit it has definitely contributed to increase awareness of the problem of corruption and arbitration and has provided further food for thought.

That said, it remains my privilege and pleasure to say thank you to many: first of all, to our two organisers, Christian Oetiker and Andrea Meier, for this excellent programme; equally to all of the panellists and moderators for their hard work and dedication to provide us with I would submit excellent speeches and presentations. I would also like to thank Robyn Nott for acting for once, not as a court reporter but as a conference reporter. Finally, I thank all of you for coming today to Geneva and for your active and lively participation.

I wish you all goodbye, safe trips back home. Some of you have come as far as Chicago and Singapore, and Moscow. I very much look forward to seeing many of you back on 13 September when we are going to have our traditional General Assembly and Conference in Berne.

Before everyone leaves, I was asked to kindly remind those who have registered that right after the conference, the arbitration flash networking event is going to take place upstairs in the hotel for all of those who still have enough energy to continue their networking activities. It is a cocktail reception organised by ASA Below 40, ASA Arbitral Women and Young Arbitral Women. Thank you again and goodbye.

## ASA SPECIAL SERIES*

1. *Le nouveau droit suisse de l'arbitrage international*, 1989.
2. *The New Swiss Law on International Arbitration*, 1990.
3. Michael E. Schneider (ed.), *Verträge und Schiedsverfahren im europäischen Umbruch*, 1990.
4. *Dispute Resolution on International Markets*, 1993.
5. *Investing in Eastern-European Countries – And Arbitration*, 1993.
6. Marc Blessing (ed.), *Objective Arbitrability – Antitrust Disputes – Intellectual Property Disputes*, 1994.
7. *Profiles of ASA Members (1994)*, 1994.
8. Marc Blessing (ed.), *The Arbitration Agreement: Its Multifold Critical Aspects*, 1994.
9. Marc Blessing (ed.), *The New York Convention of 1958*, 1996.
10. *Profiles of ASA Members (1998)*, 1998.
11. *Arbitration of Sports-Related Disputes*, 1998.
12. Pierre Karrer (ed.), *International Arbitration Do's and Don'ts*, Second Edition, 1998.
13. Pierre Karrer (ed.), *The Claims Resolution Process on Dormant Accounts in Switzerland*, 2000.
14. *Profiles of ASA Members (2000)*, 2000.
15. Pierre Karrer (ed.), *Arbitral Tribunals or State Courts: Who Must Defer to Whom?*, 2001.
16. Pierre Karrer (ed.), *Glossary of Arbitration and ADR Terms and Abbreviations*, First Edition, 2001.
17. Pierre Karrer (ed.), *International Arbitration Do's and Don'ts*, Third Edition, 2001.
18. Pierre Karrer (ed.), *Conflicts of Interest in International Commercial Arbitration*, 2001.
19. *Profiles of ASA Members (2002)*, 2002.
20. Gabrielle Kaufmann-Kohler & Viviane Frossard (eds), *Arbitration in Banking and Financial Matters*, 2003.
21. Pierre Karrer (ed.), *International Arbitration Do's and Don'ts*, Forth Edition, 2004.
22. Gabrielle Kaufmann-Kohler & Blaise Stucki (eds), *The Swiss Rules of International Arbitration*, 2004.
23. *Profiles of ASA Members (2005)*, 2005.
24. Gabrielle Kaufmann-Kohler & Alexandra Johnson (eds), *Arbitration of Merger and Acquisition Disputes*, 2005.
25. Pierre Karrer (ed.), *International Arbitration Do's and Don'ts*, Fifth Edition, 2005.
26. Markus Wirth (ed.), Best Practices in International Arbitration, 2006.

---

* Volumes 47 and onward are published by Wolters Kluwer.

27. Pierre Karrer (ed.), Glossary of Arbitration and ADR Terms and Abbreviations, Second Edition, 2006.
28. Pierre Karrer (ed.), Glossary of Arbitration and ADR Terms and Abbreviations, Third Edition, 2008.
29. Markus Wirth (ed.), *The Resolution of the Dispute, from the Hearing to the Award*, 2007.
30. Michael E. Schneider & Joachim Knoll (eds), *Performance as a Remedy: Non-Monetary Relief in International Arbitration*, 2011.
31. Pierre Karrer (ed.), *International Arbitration Do's and Don'ts*, Sixth Edition, 2009.
32. Pierre Karrer (ed.), *Glossary of Arbitration and ADR Terms and Abbreviations*, Fourth Edition, 2009.
33. *Profiles of ASA Members (2009)*, 2009.
34. Anne K. Hoffmann (ed.), *Protection of Foreign Investments through Modern Treaty Arbitration: Diversity and Harmonisation*, 2010.
35. Markus Wirth, Christina Rouvinez & Joachim Knoll (eds), *Search for "Truth" in Arbitration: Is Finding the Truth What Dispute Resolution Is About?*, 2011.
36. Elliott Geisinger & Guillaume Tattevin (eds), *Advocacy in International Commercial Arbitration*, 2013.
37. Daniele Favalli (ed.), *Sense and Non-sense of Guidelines, Rules and Other Para-regulatory Texts in International Arbitration*, 2015.
38. Pierre Tercier (ed.), *Post Award Issues*, 2012.
39. **Not published**.
40. Philipp Habegger, Daniel Hochstrasser, Gabrielle Nater-Bass & Urs Weber-Stecher (eds), Arbitral Institutions under Scrutiny, 2013.
41. Elliott Geisinger & Elena Trabaldo de Mestral (eds), *Sports Arbitration: A Coach for Other Players*, 2014.
42. Bernhard Berger & Michael E. Schneider (eds), *Inside the Black Box: How Arbitral Tribunals Operate and Reach Their Decisions*, 2013.
43. Elliott Geisinger (ed.), *Confidential and Restricted Access Information in International Arbitration*, 2016.
44. Nathalie Voser (ed.), *10 Years of Swiss Rules of International Arbitration*, 2014.
45. Domitille Baizeau & Frank Spoorenberg (eds), *Arbitrators' Initiative: When, Why and How Should It Be Used?*, 2016.
46. Sebastien Besson & Harold Frey (eds), *Expert Evidence: Conflicting Assumptions and How to Handle Them in Arbitration*, 2020.
47. Andrea Meier & Christian Oetiker (eds), *Arbitration and Corruption*, 2021.

www.ingramcontent.com/pod-product-compliance
Ingram Content Group UK Ltd.
Pitfield, Milton Keynes, MK11 3LW, UK
UKHW020843290926
15470UKWH00004B/1518

9 789403 535340